John Dewey

John Dewey

A Philosopher of Education for our time?

RICHARD PRING

Bloomsbury Library of Educational Thought
Series Editor: Richard Bailey

B L O O M S B U R Y
LONDON • NEW DELHI • NEW YORK • SYDNEY

Bloomsbury Academic
An imprint of Bloomsbury Publishing Plc

50 Bedford Square	1385 Broadway
London	New York
WC1B 3DP	NY 10018
UK	USA

www.bloomsbury.com

First published 2007 by Continuum International Publishing Group
Paperback edition first published 2014 by Bloomsbury Academic

British Library Cataloguing-in-Publication Data
A catalogue record for this book is available from the British Library.

ISBN: PB: 978-1-4725-1877-4
ePUB: 978-1-4411-2459-3

Library of Congress Cataloguing-in-Publication Data
Pring, Richard.
John Dewey/Richard Pring.
p.   cm. – (Continuum library of educational thought)
Includes bibliographical references and index.
ISBN-13: 978-0-8264-8403-1 (hardcover)
ISBN-10: 0-8264-8403-4 (hardcover)
1. Dewey, John, 1859–1952.   2. Education–Philosophy.   I. Title.   II. Series.

LB875.D5P74   2007
370.1–dc22

2007018516

Typeset by Aptara Books Ltd.

To Isaac, Eleanor, Dominic, Isobel, Lucy, Mary and Elisabette

> Now the change which is coming into our education is the shifting of the centre of gravity ... In this case the child becomes the sun about which the appliances of education revolve; he is the centre about which they are organized.
>
> (Dewey, J., *The School and Society*, p. 103)

Contents

Series Editor's Preface

Education is sometimes presented as an essentially practical activity. It is, it seems, about teaching and learning, curriculum and what goes on in schools. It is about achieving certain ends, using certain methods, and these ends and methods are often prescribed for teachers, whose duty it is to deliver them with vigor and fidelity. With such a clear purpose, what is the value of theory?

Recent years have seen politicians and policy-makers in different countries explicitly denying *any* value or need for educational theory. A clue to why this might be is offered by a remarkable comment by a British Secretary of State for Education in the 1990s: 'having any ideas about how children learn, or develop, or feel, should be seen as subversive activity'. This pithy phrase captures the problem with theory: it subverts, challenges and undermines the very assumptions on which the practice of education is based.

Educational theorists, then, are trouble-makers in the realm of ideas. They pose a threat to the status quo and lead us to question the commonsense presumptions of educational practices. But this is precisely what they should do, because the seemingly simple language of schools and schooling hides numerous contestable concepts that in their different usages reflect fundamental disagreements about the aims, values and activities of education.

Implicit within the *Bloomsbury Library of Educational Thought* is an assertion that theories and theorizing are vitally important for education. By gathering together the ideas of some of the most influential, important and interesting educational thinkers, from the ancient Greeks to contemporary scholars, the series has the ambitious task of providing an accessible yet authoritative resource for a generation of students and practitioners. Volumes within the series are written by acknowledged leaders in the field, who were selected both for their scholarship and their ability to make often complex ideas accessible to a diverse audience.

It will always be possible to question the list of key thinkers who are represented in this series. Some may question the inclusion of certain thinkers; some may disagree with the exclusion of others. That is inevitably going to be the case. There is no suggestion that the list of thinkers represented within the *Bloomsbury Library of Educational Thought* is in any way definitive. What is incontestable is that these thinkers have fascinating ideas about education, and that, taken together, the *Library* can act as a powerful source of information and inspiration for those committed to the study of education.

Richard Bailey
Roehampton University, London

Foreword

John Dewey is probably the best-known, most widely acknowledged and also the most (unfairly) maligned philosopher of education of the twentieth century. He is best known through his association with what came to be known as 'child-centered education'. His philosophical and educational writing on the aims of education (and the attention which he paid to children's interests), on the centrality of experience to education, on inquiry as the primary source of knowledge and understanding and on the importance of community to individual growth did indeed underpin many of the practices that became associated with the 'progressive education' movement of the prewar years (reflected, for example, in the work of the New Education Fellowship and its journal *New Era*, to which Dewey was a contributor). This movement itself informed the thinking that in the 1960s became enshrined in the Plowden Report on primary education and its aftermath in the UK. By the 1970s, English teachers and headteachers were being brought over to the USA to advise US teachers on the implementation of practices that had their source in the American philosopher's own educational writing.

Of course, as Richard Pring explains in this lucid and fascinating study, few of those who became enthused with what they thought Dewey had said had actually read his carefully crafted, cautious and sometimes quite difficult philosophical work. Before long, Dewey himself was having to correct and disassociate himself from the excesses into which some of his 'disciples' had fallen. His later demonization in the UK and USA by right-wing politicians (*Democracy and Education* was once listed only after *Mein Kampf* and *Das Kapital* among the most dangerous books of the twentieth century!) was the product of two layers of ignorance: ignorance of what Dewey had actually said and ignorance of the changes that had actually taken place – or, more correctly, the changes that had never really taken place on any scale – in our nations' schools. Those who read this book, with its insightful account of Dewey's philosophy and philosophy of education, will be better placed to assess both the importance that Dewey's admirers attach to his work and the level of responsibility he may or may not bear for the failings of our educational systems.

The curious thing, however, is that even as his supposed teaching was being driven out of more narrowly defined educational circles in the last quarter of the twentieth century, the same teaching was surfacing in other ways. 'Child-centered education' may have been pushed out of the school system, but 'student-centered learning' and 'learner-centered learning' was in, and has remained so to this day, in adult and continuing education. Project-based learning might have lost its place in the primary school, but project- and problem-based learning – preferably constructed around real-life problems – was becoming *de rigueur* in vocational and professional training. Dewey's pragmatism might be out of fashion, but Kolb's experiential learning cycle, which was only a simplified and schematized version of this pragmatism, was referenced in almost every 'training the trainers' manual. Action research, enthusiastically espoused by the teaching profession in many parts of the world, and benignly endorsed by many ministries of education, was essentially constructed on a pragmatic view of knowledge and its development. In learning theory, in curriculum discourse and in the rapidly expanding arena of qualitative research in education, a combination of Dewey's pragmatism and the social psychological work of his long-standing colleague, George Herbert Mead, provided and continues to provide perhaps the most frequently employed conceptual framing. Today, in both the USA and the UK, government funders apply the apparently pragmatic demand to educational research that it should tell them 'what works' – though if Dewey were alive today, he would probably be writing furiously to disassociate himself from this particular corruption of his epistemology.

There can be no doubt, I think, that even as we approach the centenary of the publication of *Democracy and Education*, the continuing relevance of Dewey's writing is everywhere to be seen. But the history of the treatment or mistreatment of his philosophical and educational

work indicates that if we are to benefit from his real insights, then we
need to take some trouble to understand their philosophical ground.
Richard Pring, a distinguished philosopher and educator who has
had a long-standing interest in Dewey's work, is admirably equipped
to lead us into both his philosophical writing and his educational
thought. This is an excellent introduction, which demonstrates very
clearly that John Dewey is indeed 'a philosopher for our time'.

Professor David Bridges
Von Hügel Institute, St Edmund's College,
Cambridge and University of East Anglia

Introduction: Genesis and Nature
of the Book

As an undergraduate in philosophy at University College London, I sat in the library opposite the collected works of John Dewey. I was vaguely curious about this man. How could a person write so much and yet be read so little? His name was never mentioned in my three-year course in philosophy. No one was ever known to have borrowed or to have read anything from this vast literature within its dusty covers. His sole claim to fame seemed to be that he was held responsible (wrongly) for the quaint way in which his books were classified.

In some respects, this is strange. Bertrand Russell's *History of Western Philosophy*, first published in 1946, refers to Dewey as 'generally admitted to be the leading living philosopher of America'. Robert Westbrook, in his book *John Dewey and American Democracy*, says of Dewey that he 'would become the most important philosopher in modern American history, honored and attacked by men and women all over the world' (p. ix). Misconceived though Dewey may be thought to have been, especially (in the judgment of Russell) in his concept of 'truth', he was seen to be of immense importance and influence, certainly in the USA.

That distinction of being the 'leading living philosopher of America' lay partly in the 'pragmatic theory of meaning', through which so many baffling philosophical problems were claimed to have been solved. That 'pragmatism' was deeply influential on the social psychological work of George Herbert Mead, who was a colleague of Dewey at the University of Michigan, and then at Chicago, and whose theoretical account of how personal identity is formed through social interaction ('symbolic interaction') continues to influence educational research, within an ethnographic tradition, to this day. Dewey was both influenced by and influenced Mead. But despite this important influence of pragmatism, Russell deals most cursorily with the 'father of pragmatism', C.S. Peirce, who gets only a two-line mention (in the chapter on Dewey) and a similarly brief mention in the chapter on William James.

Perhaps that is why Dewey did not attain the recognition in Britain that clearly he received in the USA. I did read C.S. Peirce. He was on the syllabus. But pragmatism never became part of the central philosophical tradition, perhaps because, according to Russell (1946b, p. 774), the 'substitution of 'inquiry' for 'truth' as the fundamental concept of logic and theory of knowledge' was simply not acceptable.

Much more recently, an interest in Dewey within Britain has been stimulated by Alan Ryan's *John Dewey and the High Tide of American Liberalism* (1995). This places the philosophical, political and educational writings of Dewey within the broader context of his life and the political and social life of the USA. And, indeed, that makes sense, because, as Ryan argues, Dewey's writings were a reflection on, a making sense of, an engagement with that social context, with a view to 'intelligent action'.

His educational writings, even when his more strictly philosophical ones seemed to be ignored, were immensely influential, especially within what was called the 'progressive movement' in the United States. 'The project method', written in 1918 by W.H. Kilpatrick, a colleague of Dewey at Columbia University, translated Dewey's educational ideas into a curriculum in which the practical and interdisciplinary *project* provided the relevant interest to motivate the learner, while initiating the learner into the different kinds of knowledge relevant to the project's solution. But, ironically, one test of the strength of ideas is the degree to which they are judged to be the source of subsequent evils. The economic difficulties faced by the USA in the 1970s against increased economic challenges from Japan and other overseas competitors were placed firmly at the door of the educational system, and particularly of the ideas of 'progressive educationalists', the leading one having been (according to the critics) John Dewey. As Nell Noddings says, in *Philosophy of Education*, not only has he:

been hailed as the savior of American education by those who welcome greater involvement of students in their own planning and
activity [but also] he has been called 'worse than Hitler' by some
who felt that he infected schools with epistemological and moral
relativism and substituted socialization for true education.

(Noddings, 2005)

Larry Cuban (2004), in *The Blackboard and the Bottom Line: Why Schools
Can't Be Businesses*, describes the reversal to a business model with a
high-stakes assessment regime, the very antithesis of the educational
ideals of Dewey.

However, this attribution to Dewey of the purported evils of 'progressive education' was mistaken. Dewey was himself a thoroughgoing critic of much that fell under that title. But such an attribution
reflects the way in which educational thinking is so easily translated
into slogans. As Scheffler argues in *The Language of Education,*

[t]he example of John Dewey's educational influence is instructive.
His systematic, careful, and qualified statements soon were translated into striking segments serving as slogans for the new progressive tendencies in American education. Dewey himself criticized the
uses to which some of his ideas were put.

(1960, p. 37)

Critics of educational developments in postwar Britain similarly attach
much of the blame for the perceived perversity of 'child-centeredness'
on the influence of Dewey. Frequent reference is made to him from
within what might be called the progressive tradition. He was identified by Brian Simon as one of the influences upon 'the primary
school "revolution" which emerged in the 1930s', and which became
part of the 'ideological orthodoxy' behind the Plowden Report of
1967 (Simon, 1991, p. 362). Indeed, when I came to Oxford in
1989, I was seated at dinner next to Lord Keith Joseph, who had
been Secretary of State for Education under Prime Minister Mar-
garet Thatcher. He accused me of being responsible for all the
problems in our schools – because I had introduced teachers to
John Dewey. And subsequently there was a systematic attack on
Dewey the educator even from philosophers as well as journalists

and politicians. Professor O'Hear, for example, proposed that '[i]t is highly plausible to see the egalitarianism which stems from the writings of John Dewey as the proximate cause of our educational decline' (1991, p. 28).

On the other hand, just as it was difficult to find anyone who had read Dewey as a philosopher, so too it was difficult, at least in Britain, to find anyone who had read him as an educator. Frequent reference was indeed made to him by leading philosophers of education both in the USA and Britain (Peters, 1981, in his *Essays on Educators*, gives a sympathetic but ultimately critical account), and several weeks were devoted to the study of *Democracy and Education* by the research group of the Institute of Education in the London Institute of Education in 1970. The American Educational Research Association (AERA) has an active subgroup of educational researchers devoted to the critical study of John Dewey. But such minority academic interest hardly constituted a radicalization of teachers. And so it is difficult to see how his writings actually changed minds, or entered into the practical development of education – except through the 'philosophy' that permeated the colleges of education which trained the teachers.

On the other hand, Darling (1994), in his book *Child-Centred Education and Its Critics*, gives a detailed account of a two-pronged attack on the ideas which were associated (often wrongly) with Dewey. First, the 'revolution in philosophy' (the title of Gilbert Ryle's book, 1956) came to dominate the philosophy of education at the very time when, in Britain, educational studies aimed to become a respectable academic discipline. In similar vein, the philosophy of education in North America was also 'revolutionized' by the work of philosophers such as Israel Scheffler, whose book *The Language of Education* had wide influence. This 'revolution' understood the task of philosophy as one not of giving answers to substantial questions about, say, the aims of education or about how one should teach, but of providing second-order logical analysis of what was *meant* by 'education' (and its aims) or by the concept of teaching. Hence, the 'new philosophy' was vehemently critical of those educational prescriptions which often went under the name of philosophy. Archambault (a North American exponent of the revolution in philosophy of education) spoke of 'the need to clean the stables' and referred to 'the failure, on the part of philosophers of education to recognise or to use the gains made in recent philosophy' (1965, p. 8).

Philosophy clarifies but does not prescribe. The 'revolutionaries' at the Institute of Education in London, led by Professor Richard Peters, focused particularly upon the claims of what was referred to as the child-centered tradition. That included John Dewey, and the way in which 'growth' or 'self-realization', it was argued, constituted the aim of education in different versions of child-centered education. It was such a claim that received the full onslaught of the analytic philosophers such as Dearden (see *The Philosophy of Primary Education*, 1968, pp. 37ff.) and Peters (see *Education and the Education of Teachers*, 1977). Dewey, *qua* philosopher, sought to change practice. That, according to the revolutionized philosophy of education, was not acceptable – unless, of course, practice changed simply as a result of thinking clearly about it. The new orthodoxy had little room for Dewey and the educational thinking that he stood for – a matter that will be returned to in Chapter 3.

Second, the philosophical attack coincided with an increasing disillusionment on the part of the Conservative government in Britain and of the federal government in the United States with the standards and effectiveness of schools. Given the philosophical criticism of what was comprehensively called child-centered education, this was seen to be the cause of all the ills. Therefore, in both North America and in Britain there was an attack on so-called progressive education, a call for more formal methods of teaching and a demand for more systematic assessment of what had been learned. The villain of the piece was so often seen as being John Dewey.

Nonetheless, those who do read Dewey's extensive works will find them challenging and, given the continuing failure of the educational system to engage so many reluctant learners, persuasive. It is worth asking once again if he is a philosopher of education for our time.

On the other hand, his philosophical views so permeate his educational thinking that it is difficult to see how one can accept the latter where one finds difficulty with the philosophical theory of pragmatism – where, for example, one is sympathetic to Russell's view that error lies in the substitution of 'inquiry' for 'truth' as the fundamental concept in a theory of knowledge. However persuasive Dewey's educational writings appear to be, there is an interweaving of these with his philosophical views such that it is not easy to accept the educational recommendations without accepting, too, a philosophical position that one might otherwise find unacceptable.

To meet this difficulty, the book is divided into four further parts following Part 1, which introduces Dewey's life and writings. Part 2 looks directly at the key ideas that shaped Dewey's educational thinking and practice. Philosophical issues will necessarily arise, but a systematic philosophical exposition of these will be postponed to Part 3. There an attempt will be made to expose the underlying philosophical position, namely that of pragmatism (or Dewey's version of it, 'experimentalism' or 'instrumentalism'). Finally, in Part 4 I shall put the two together – and see what can be salvaged.

The nature of Dewey's philosophical views gives one confidence in writing about them. To explain this, I need to anticipate what I shall be saying later about his philosophy of pragmatism. For pragmatism is essentially a theory of meaning. The meaning of a word, or a sentence, or a whole text lies in the practical effects it has. Of course, such practical effects must be shaped by the text as it is reflected upon; it must be disciplined by the words that the text contains. But nonetheless, the meaning of the text lies in those effects. Furthermore, those effects on me, albeit determined to some extent by the contexts and interests from which I approach the text, lie in a transformation of how I see and think about what Dewey said. It is at times difficult to distinguish in Dewey between the meaning of a text *as such* and the meaning *for me*. Hence, in giving an account of Dewey and having read carefully the text, I am (and am entitled so to do) giving an account of its meaning for me (its *effect*), and this in turn may well help 'reconstruct' others' reconstructions, thereby becoming part of the meaning of what he said.

Anyone trying to get to grips with what Dewey said about education would need to tackle certain key ideas that seemed to shape his thinking. I have picked out seven of these. They produce the perspective through which his abundant writing might be understood – although many may disagree with these as the key ones, and thus with my interpretation of Dewey. These ideas are:

- educational aims (and the interests, discipline and growth of the child)
- experience (and thinking about and reflection upon experience)
- inquiry (and what understanding and truth mean)
- child-centeredness
- knowledge and the subject matter of the curriculum
- community (and the place of the individual within it)
- schooling (and its relation to society).

In a paper I wrote in 1987, I referred to Dewey as the likely 'patron saint of TVEI' (the Technical and Vocational Education Initiative) (Pring, 1989). This was a program launched by the Manpower Services Commission of the UK's Department of Employment in 1983. It emphasized more practical and experiential learning, a learning that challenged the divisive and 'false' dualism between academic and vocational studies and that insisted upon greater relevance to the wider community of what is learned. The popularity of that program throughout the country did not gain it survival beyond the launch of the National Curriculum in Britain in 1988. But even if the authors and creators of TVEI had never read Dewey, Dewey would, I think, have recognized his educational ideas in much of the TVEI practice. And he would have recognized, too, the rejection of his ideas and ideals by those who rejected TVEI in welcoming the National Curriculum.

This book, therefore, is really concerned with the ideas that underpin educational practice – about the ideological struggle for the aims of education as these are embedded in educational practices. In trying to identify these and articulate them, I do so with Dewey in mind, but no doubt I frequently stray beyond what can be strictly justified by the many texts. But that worries me no more than it would worry Dewey were he still alive. For, according to him, the meaning of what is said or written lies in the effects that it has. The writings of Dewey help me to 'reconstruct' my understanding of educational practice – as indeed I hope my interpretation would transform his in the never-ending growth of understanding, which, according to Dewey, has no finale.

Part 1

Intellectual Biography

Chapter 1

Dewey: The Man, his Life, his Writings and his Bequest

Chicago and Columbia University, New York

In 122nd Street, Manhattan, stands the prestigious Columbia University, New York. For 26 years, John Dewey was professor of philosophy there. But for him the distinction between philosophizing and thinking about education was very blurred. His *philosophical* analysis of 'experience' was central to his *educational* thinking, and his central educational aim of 'growth' was intimately tied to a pragmatic theory of meaning and value. Hence, the large hall in which he lectured was as full with educational students as it was with budding philosophers. And it was, and is, a large hall. Therefore, even if not many read his many educational works, many generations of teachers were influenced by his educational thinking. Indeed, his influence did not stop when he retired. He continued to write, tour and lecture almost till his death in 1952. It was during this period at Columbia that he wrote *Democracy and Education* (1916), which set out his educational philosophy most completely.

Prior to that period, Dewey had been for ten years head of the Department of Philosophy, Psychology and Pedagogy at the University of Chicago. He had been appointed in 1894, at the age of 35. Such was the significance of his philosophical thinking that the philosopher William James was inspired to say:

Chicago has a School of Thought! – a school of thought, which it is safe to predict, will figure in literature as the School of Chicago for twenty-five years to come. Some universities have plenty of thought to show, but no school; others have plenty of school, but no thought. The University of Chicago, by its Decennial Publications, shows real

thought and a real school. Professor John Dewey, and at least ten
of his disciples, have collectively put into the world a statement,
homogeneous in spite of so many cooperating minds, of a view
of the world, both theoretical and practical, which is so simple,
massive, and positive that, in spite of the fact that many parts of it
yet need to be worked out, it deserves the title of a new system of
philosophy.

(James, 1904, p. 172)

The publications referred to included a paper by Dewey on logical
theory and one by George Herbert Mead on 'the definition of the
psychical'.

However, these ten years, before he moved in 1904 to Columbia
University, New York, saw the parallel development of Dewey as
philosopher and educator. The two, as I have said, were so closely
integrated that it is difficult to separate them. His educational books
written while he was at Chicago – *School and Society* and *The Child
and the Curriculum* – embodied the principles that were made explicit
in the philosophical guide to teachers, *How We Think* (published in
1910, after he left Chicago, but written mainly while he was there).
Again one sees here the close connection between doing philosophy
and thinking about education. In a way, these are not two separate
activities. In thinking about the purpose of what you are doing educationally, you are necessarily thinking about the purposes of education, about the values that inform practice, and about the nature of
the knowledge and experience transmitted, and these are essentially
philosophical activities. Moreover, such thinking cannot be aloof from
practice; it is a making sense of practice with a view to improving upon
it. And so that thinking had to be embedded in the practice of teaching. At Chicago, therefore, Dewey established, with his wife, a university elementary school, of which he was the director. This was integral
to the university and to its activities in the preparation of teachers.

Intellectual influences

Before we examine the beliefs that shaped Dewey's educational
thinking in Chicago and, consistently, for the rest of his long life,

it is important to speak briefly of his life before his appointment in Chicago and of the key philosophical influences upon his own development.

Dewey was born in Burlington, Vermont, in 1859. At the age of 16 he went to the University of Vermont, where he read Darwin's *The Origin of Species* (published in 1859) and engaged with the arguments which arose from that publication. Evolutionary theory remained a powerful influence on Dewey's philosophical, and therefore educational, thinking. Philosophically, it helped solve the dualism of mind and body, which, in different ways, was the basis of the errors he attributed to both rationalist and empiricist traditions. Human beings are but a higher form of biological organism, with innate purposes and, therefore, with purposive adaptation to the environment, which, however, included the social environment of human interaction and culture.

Having graduated from Vermont in 1879, Dewey taught for three years in a couple of schools, not very successfully, before entering Johns Hopkins University for graduate studies in philosophy. One colleague was Charles Sanders Peirce, who is generally recognized to be the 'founding father' of 'pragmatism', although he renamed it 'pragmaticism' – a term so ugly that the likes of Dewey and William James were unlikely to steal it. At Johns Hopkins University, Dewey also encountered the influence of Hegelian idealism, partly through his senior colleague George Morris and partly through his subsequent acquaintance with the Oxford idealists F.H Bradley and T.H. Green. Hegel's philosophy 'supplied a demand for unification that was doubtless an intense emotional craving, and yet was a hunger that only an intellectualized subject-matter could satisfy' (quoted in Westbrook, 1991, p. 14).

To put very briefly and inadequately the significance of this upon Dewey's formation, one might say that Dewey's 'demand for unification' resulted in his belief, first, in the essential connectedness of all experience; second, in the constructive role of the mind in discovering that interconnectedness; and third, in the consequent dissolving of the dualism between the 'spectating mind' and the 'spectated world'. Life was to be regarded as an 'organism', but, as far as human beings are concerned, not in the purely biological sense; the ideas and purposes that are somehow immanent in the human organism come to fruition or realize themselves through experience.

In 1884, Dewey followed Morris to the University of Michigan, where eventually, in 1889, he became head of the philosophy department. There his idealist sympathies developed into social thinking, much influenced by his reading of T.H. Green (see, for example, Dewey's account of this in 'The philosophy of Thomas Hill Green' in the *Andover Review* in 1889). Two features of this social thinking that are particularly relevant to his later educational ideas were, first, the central role of philosophy in helping to understand and to tackle the problems of public and social life, and, second, the ethical value of the freedom of persons to make the best of themselves. That 'making the best of themselves' took place within a social context – a community in which the best interests of each would be the best interests of all.

Prior, then, to his appointment at Chicago, we can see the main elements emerging which led William James to say that 'Chicago had a School of Thought': the idea of each 'human organism' growing through adaptation to the social environment; that adaptation being purposive as each person seeks meaning in his or her experience; that adaptation taking place through interaction with other persons who in turn are trying to make sense of their experience; the context of that interaction being the community of individuals that is created by those interactions and in turn affects them; the ultimate aim (the end in the ethical sense) of this purposive adaptation being the growing capacity to adapt to and to benefit from these interactive experiences; and, finally, the social agenda being that of engaging with the problems of community life. Education, then, becomes the facilitation of this growth and adaptation.

Five core beliefs

At the core of educational philosophy that inspired the establishment of the University Elementary School were five beliefs which shaped his thinking for over 50 years and which received little modification. These beliefs, set out in 1897 in 'My pedagogic creed', written shortly after his appointment at Chicago, were a considered reaction to what Dewey saw to be the traditional way in which education, so called, was conducted. Such traditional education was seen

- to be disconnected from the experiences that the students brought from their homes and their community
- to be disconnected from the practical and manual activity through which they are engaged with experience
- to ignore the interests that motivated young people to learn
- to treat knowledge as something purely symbolic and formal – organized in textbooks, 'stuck on' without connections to experience or existing ways of understanding
- to maintain discipline through external authority rather than through the engagement of the young people.

The solutions offered in the Laboratory School (see below) were a reaction to such a traditional conception of education.

First, the school should be an extension of the home and the community, bringing greater system to the acquisition of that understanding which is essential, or at least very useful, for daily living. Much practical knowledge is, of course, picked up informally in family and community, but the school's aim should be to deepen that understanding, to enable the young people to reflect upon it, and to enhance its value – to return to home and community with something to offer and to enhance the understanding of both.

Second, in being an extension of the experience of the home and the community, the school should value manual and practical activity, which, after all, is an essential and meaningful part of that domestic and communal life. It is through such practical and manual activities as carpentry (we are now thinking about Chicago in the early twentieth century), sewing, cooking and weaving that one understands the basis of ordinary survival and living – something too often forgotten by those who theorize about the human condition.

Third, the interests of young people were to be treated as of importance in their own right, not simply as something that can be harnessed to the aims of the teacher for the purpose of motivating them to do things that they are not really interested in. The *interests themselves* need to be educated – the driving force to further learning.

Fourth, although school subjects at their best represent the organization of knowledge that we have inherited, they are but useful
organizations, produced to help us act intelligently in the world.
Their value lies in their usefulness – as resources upon which one
might draw to tackle questions that rarely fit neatly into the logical
boundaries set by the different subjects.

Fifth, a young person whose interests are taken seriously and whose
teacher seeks to develop those interests (that is, to enable the young
person to engage with them more intelligently and reflectively) will
be disciplined by the pursuit of those interests – making the regime
of externally imposed discipline irrelevant.

Therefore, the school is to be seen not simply as an extension of
the wider community but as a community in itself, and the student
is seen as an active member of that community. The behavioral discipline arises not from externally imposed sanctions but from the
internalized norms of living within such a community.

Thus, behind Dewey's experimental school was a particular view
of the normal young learner: someone who is curious and interested, but whose curiosity and interests had been sapped by modes
of learning which took no account of that *interest* in learning. Rather,
the schools should reflect upon the process of inquiry and ensure
that the expertise of the teacher and the cultural resources available
through teachers were made available to young people as they were
encouraged to pursue those interests. However, such interests, within
the right kind of school community, would embrace, too, the wider
needs of the community to which the individuals belonged.

Dewey's approach to pedagogy was essentially experimental, as one
might have expected, given that 'experimentalism' was one name
given subsequently to his own distinctive philosophical position. Ideas
had to be tried out and tested in practice. Therefore, the establishment of a school for testing out ideas – what came to be called the
'Laboratory School' – seemed to be essential. All this was before
teacher training was introduced to the University of Chicago with
the transfer to the university of the Chicago Institute of Education in
1901, which already had a 'training school' attached to it. Inevitably
there was some confusion between the place of the two schools within
the overall faculty and program. The Laboratory School did not

survive Dewey's departure to Columbia University in 1904 – but the ideas did.

Those ideas – to be developed further in subsequent chapters of this book – might be contrasted with the practice that was generally current, namely elementary education as very largely the transmission of information. Dewey saw it, rather, as an active engagement with a problem, with identifying a way forward, with the testing out of that 'hypothesis', with the community as a resource for thinking through the problem. Those problems were partly social, namely how to live in harmony with different people pursuing different, although often interacting, interests. Part of being educated lay in working harmoniously with others in the school community, benefiting from their ideas and experience. The school was a mini-society.

Dewey left the University of Chicago to go to Columbia University, New York, in 1904. No doubt, however, the University of Chicago remained much influenced by the ten-year presence of John Dewey. Indeed, it became one of the major centers of educational studies in the world, closely related to the practice of education, as is reflected in the work of Philip Jackson, whose *Life in Classrooms* (1968) influenced generations of teachers. But that School of Education exists no longer. Anxious to prove itself academically, it withdrew from the daily contact with classrooms to find time to write and publish research. At the same time, that research did not seem to meet the standards of the School of Sociology to which it became attached. Bereft of friends in schools, which could not see its professional relevance, and bereft of friends in the university, which could not detect its academic merit, it finally closed. If only that school had hearkened to the warning voice of its 'old boy', John Dewey, for whom the separation of theory from practice distorted theory and impoverished practice. (Would the present architects of the Research Assessment Exercise in Britain please take note?)

At Teachers College of Columbia University in New York, Dewey spent the rest of his long academic life. His most important work from the point of view of education, *Democracy and Education*, was published while he was there, in 1916. It is a long book, the difficult prose of which is alleviated by very useful summaries at the end of each chapter. Nonetheless, like all long and difficult books, it was open to misinterpretation. And so, over 20 years later, in 1938, Dewey wrote a much shorter book, *Experience and Education*, which explained how his work should not be so readily harnessed to any 'ism', especially 'progressivism'. Indeed, the job of the philosopher of education was not to side with either one of the warring parties ('traditionalists' or 'progressives'), nor indeed to seek a *via media* between them, but to introduce 'a new order of conceptions leading to new modes of practice' (p. 5).

It is his attempt to do this that makes Dewey so relevant today. Too often the conflicts about educational practice, reflected in educational language, are seen in terms of the very dualities that Dewey vigorously opposed: academic versus vocational, theory versus practice, work versus leisure, school versus society, and (yes, still) traditional subject-based versus inquiry-based or interest-based learning. Perhaps we, too, need to find, in the light of what Dewey had to say, 'a new order of conceptions leading to new modes of practice'.

That 'new order of conceptions' is to be found in a set of writings, which are *mainly* educational and *all* philosophical, published during Dewey's 30 or so years at Chicago and Columbia. For the purposes of this book, I draw particularly upon the following for his most directly educational thinking:

'My pedagogic creed', 1897, in *The School Journal*, 14 (3)
The School and Society, three lectures given in 1899 and published in 1900, with a revised edition in 1915, namely 'School and social progress', 'The school and the life of the child' and 'Waste in education'
The Child and the Curriculum, 1902
How We Think, 1910
Democracy and Education, 1916
Experience and Education, 1938

I draw upon the following for his more specifically philosophical thinking, which provides the foundation to the educational proposals:

Reconstruction in Philosophy, 1920
Experience and Nature, 1925
Logic: the Theory of Inquiry, 1938

The wider influence of John Dewey on other key writers (philosophers, sociologists and educationalists) is not developed in this book, although it would be an interesting and valuable task for someone to map out that influence. However, it would, I think, be true to say that the influence of Dewey on George Herbert Mead (and vice versa) was deep and significant, as was the influence of Mead on subsequent generations of sociologists of education. The 'symbolic interactionism' that characterized Mead's analysis of social relations is firmly within the pragmatic tradition of Peirce and Dewey, whose junior colleague he was. And that in turn had a profound impact upon generations of sociologists and educational researchers in North America and Britain. That indirect influence of Dewey is rarely acknowledged, even by the proponents of 'action research', which has proved to be so popular – the way forward, as it were, for 'school improvement'. But, as David Bridges (2004) points out in his recent book, the pragmatic theory of meaning of Dewey lay behind the theory of action research of Lewin and his disciples, and thus that theory, with all the problems it contains, needs to be recognized by those who engage in the practice of action research.

Part 2

Critical Exposition of Dewey's Work

Chapter 2

Educational Aims

Problems of definition

In *Democracy and Education,* Dewey 'reaches a technical definition of education'. It is that 'reconstruction or reorganization of experience which adds to the meaning of experience, and which increases ability to direct the course of subsequent experience' (p. 76). There are many other statements in *Democracy and Education* about what education is, but they are but extensions or articulations of what is meant by this central definition. However, before this definition is explained, perhaps it would be helpful to reflect a little on what is meant by a definition. What exactly is Dewey doing?

To define a word is to expose its meaning, and the meaning lies in its use within a language. To define a word, therefore, is not simply to give alternative words, but to show how a word is used, the rules for its usage, and its place in a particular form of discourse. Hence, certain words have several meanings, insofar as they are used in different ways in different contexts. The differences I refer to are not those where a word is used in quite equivocal senses (as, for example, where 'plane' refers both to something that flies and to a carpenter's tool). Rather do the differences in usage still have overlapping meanings. There can be a range of different usages of a word, giving rise to different definitions, albeit within a broad 'family of resemblances'.

'Education' is one such word. It is applied differently by different people (one person's idea of an educated person may not be another's), but there are certain common features in its many different applications. One common feature concerns the promotion of learning in one way or another. And it applies to people, not to dogs or horses. Why? Because it is people rather than animals who are able to acquire the conceptual grasp of situations that enables them to respond appropriately – something more, and other, than a purely behavioral response. Such learning leads to further learning such that there is *growth of capacity* through increased knowledge, understanding and skill. Of course, there are some who would want to deny this distinction and talk about the education, not just the training, of animals. But, if so, they are diminishing the gap between animals and humans, attributing to animals the qualities normally attributed to human beings. Education implies growth of learning – and learning that goes beyond behavior modification.

Furthermore, there is frequently an *evaluative* ring to our use of 'education'. In being educated, one is in some way *improving*, becoming more able to do what it is proper to do. One is enriched in some way. Hence, we do talk, as a compliment, of someone being 'an educated person'. He or she has acquired certain capacities that enrich and increase competence.

One could say therefore that education has both a descriptive and an evaluative meaning. In the descriptive sense, it refers to the learning that takes place, and in the evaluative sense it implies that this kind of learning is good and capacity-building. But even in the descriptive sense, it is difficult to erase completely the evaluative use or meaning of the word. Schools are seen as educational institutions not just because they are places formally constituted to help young people to learn, but because the learning that takes place is generally regarded as being of value and as developing the capacity to think, and that is regarded as a worthwhile objective. If such a school were seen, instead, to be indoctrinating in a particular creed and thereby curbing the capacity to think, then one would say that, despite the fact that something was being learned, the young people were not being educated.

For that reason, certain kinds of organized learning that might *descriptively* be called education might very well be regarded as not educational in the *evaluative* sense.

Contrasting conceptions of education

What I have done in the foregoing remarks is to give a very basic analysis of the meaning of the word 'education' – how the word is used, both descriptively and evaluatively. I have refrained from the more detailed analysis that philosophers of education provided when the 'revolution in philosophy', referred to in the Introduction, began to stiffen the thinking in education. Peters (1966) set out the criteria, derived from usage, by which an activity can be correctly called 'educational', namely that it leads to the development of knowledge and understanding, that the knowledge is not narrow but gives a wider 'cognitive perspective', and that the knowledge is regarded as worthwhile. In setting out these criteria, the analytic philosophers would claim that they are doing no more than analyzing how the concept is used within our language – how the world is 'mapped out' in the language we employ. Philosophy is a second-order activity. Nothing follows, so it was claimed, from such an analysis, about what in fact is worthwhile or how one ought to teach.

The criticism of Dewey from such a philosophical camp was, therefore, twofold. First, Dewey had very positive things to say about what to teach and what is worth learning. He went beyond what could be claimed as a philosopher. Second, that which he claimed to be worthwhile – namely, the transformation or reconstruction of experience, self-realization, growth – did not survive the scalpel of philosophical analysis. 'Growth' cannot be an end in itself; its value lies in the end product to which the growth is leading up to.

Had Dewey been alive to respond to these criticisms, he would have pointed to the fact that his critics, under the guise of a 'second-order activity', had a substantive educational agenda of their own – a perception of what counted as an educated person which could not be derived from the usage of the word itself. The educated person was someone who had been initiated into the distinctive forms of knowledge that constituted what it means to think, to inquire and to reason. This was developed most effectively in Britain by a colleague of R.S. Peters, Professor Paul Hirst, in his paper 'Liberal education and the nature of knowledge' (1965), which provided the philosophical basis of the influential work of Her Majesty's Inspectorate in defining the eight areas of experience which the curriculum needed to cover. Similar influential papers were written in the USA by educational philosophers such as Scheffler (1965) and Schwab (1964). These forms of knowledge could be analyzed into their key and distinctive concepts, modes of verification and methods of inquiry. Hence, from the so-called analysis of the concept, substantive proposals were made for the curriculum – ones that were different from those of John Dewey.

Dewey, by contrast, focuses, not on a specific outcome of learning – namely, the different forms of knowledge and the logical structure, the divisions of which are defined by philosophers and become the subject matter to be transmitted – but upon the 'process of growth' of a living organism. Such 'growth' arises from interaction with the environment. That environment is social as well as physical, and so a purely biological conception of 'growth' would be misplaced. As he says in *The Child and the Curriculum* (CC; see the bibliography of Dewey's works at the end of the book for abbreviations),

> The fundamental factors in the educative process are an immature, undeveloped being; and certain social aims, meanings, values incarnate in the matured experience of the adult. The educative process is the due interaction of these forces. Such a conception of each in relation to the other as facilitates completest and freest interaction is the essence of educational theory.
>
> (CC, p. 123)

That growth, or 'educative process', which arises from the interaction between an 'immature, undeveloped being' and the environment, including the social environment of the mature adult, involves not just more of the same (like a river, which simply gets bigger) but a 'transformation' of what one previously was. One thinks, experiences and feels differently. 'Experience is transformed.' One's understanding of the world is 'reconceptualized' – not just new ideas added on. And this transformation takes place not always or necessarily at the conscious level. Habits are transformed; skills are enhanced, making adaptation to the newly understood environment more effective, and thus giving rise to further possible transformations of experience. If one were to talk about the ends of the process of education, then it would be in terms of yet more growth and greater capacity to adapt, not the acquisition of particular, well-defined (by universities, examination boards or government) forms of knowledge. But, in fact, there is no end to this continuing transformation. Education has 'as its aim at every stage an added capacity for growth' (DE, p. 54). That growth has no end, except in death.

For Dewey, therefore, certain experiences would be non-educational, or even miseducational, insofar as they blocked further experiences or stultified the mind – even though they were part of the 'educational system' and even though they were, both in content and in intention, introducing young people to the different forms of knowledge. That is why Dewey throughout his writings is so critical of what he refers to as 'traditional education' – that is, the systematic transmission of knowledge (education in the descriptive sense) which fails to transform the way in which young people think, feel, experience and believe in their daily lives (education in the evaluative sense). For example, rote learning of tables in arithmetic might be regarded as part of one's education *descriptively* (it was part of the learning experience of the school), but it may be regarded as *miseducational* in the evaluative sense of the word, because (and this would no doubt be disputed) such rote learning inhibited understanding.

What, then, according to Dewey, is it that makes some experiences educational and others not so?

First, as has already been said, those experiences are not educational, and indeed might be regarded as miseducational, which do not lead to, or which get in the way of, further experiences – which block the mind, as it were, through boredom or fear or indoctrination. The student cramming for an examination in literature might be so put off ever reading literature again that, even if he or she receives a good mark, the experience could be regarded as *mis*educational.

Second, the educational aspect or value of those experiences lies in the development of the distinctive nature of human beings, namely their capacity to experience the world (of which they are part, but from which they are to some extent independent), not simply as a physical response to it but as enabling them to cope with the world. The experience changes the capacity to deal more usefully with further experiences – to anticipate, to plan and to create experiences, so that yet further experiences can be generated and capacity to cope with the world enlarged. An experience is, therefore, a conceptualization of that world, an internalization of it, which affects both further experiences and the capacity to handle these. Those further experiences both transform and are transformed by previous experiences, leading to changes in the capacity to anticipate and deal with future experiences.

A simple illustration of this would be the child who has been bitten by a dog. This transforms the child's previous experience of dogs. The meaning of 'dog' becomes more complex. It is not only a creature that can be friendly and cuddly; it is one that can also be angry and dangerous. This transformation of experience changes the child's future behavior; it prepares him or her for further experiences, leaving the child more able to anticipate danger and to handle new experiences. A very young child has too limited a set of experiences to survive. Early education lies in the gaining and transformation of experiences that enable it to survive and to obtain some mastery of the environment. A childhood that limits the range of experiences prevents the child from anticipating and dealing with further experiences – possibly with danger thereby to survival.

That internalization of experience – that transformation of existing capacity to experience – might not be at the conscious level. Indeed, it might transform habits and skills – the way one instinctively relates to the environment and also the dexterity with which one is able to respond. Furthermore, the development of consciously experiencing the world might arise from a reflection on the 'know-how', the practical ability that is embodied in habits and skills. The cyclist has such 'know-how'. He or she, through prior experiences, has internalized the capacity to respond to new experiences – to balance, to brake, to turn, and to increase speed appropriately. Such a capacity will evolve through further experience (skidding on ice, for example) without that evolution being fully represented at the conscious level, although it could be consciously represented (it could be theorized about) and thereby made to affect the capacity in a different way.

Within such an analysis, and indeed within the definition above, is the notion of 'meaning'. What does Dewey signify by that? In answering, we are moving into fairly deep philosophical territory which I shall deal with more explicitly in Part 3. Let us here see 'meaning' as what experience does for you, how it enables you to act upon the world and to anticipate what will happen. The meaning of an experience lies in its effect upon action. For example, the meaning of mathematics to the young person may be different from its meaning for the professional mathematician. It *means* boredom, frustration, a sense of failure. Those may well be the experiences as a result of doing mathematics. In that case the experience is *miseducational*. It terminates what might have been an interest in mathematics. It thus undermines the capacity to experience the world in a more fruitful way.

Social dimension of education

Both the formation and the transformation of experiences is a social matter in three senses.

First, without being born into a social group, the child would not have the opportunity to acquire the further experience that can be internalized and that enables him or her to survive. Furthermore, much of these early years will consist of that gradual sophistication of experience related to surviving and to growing in a particular society. Where a society is relatively primitive, this education can take place within the family and village community. The child will learn the skills of survival: hunting, making tools and using them. Those skills can become sophisticated through constant practice and trial and error, as the conditions in which they take place and the experiences themselves change. Thus, experience presents new problems, which provide new stimulus to think through, which in turn creates new ideas – new reorganizations of experience which are then tested out – leading to new formulations.

Second, the transformation is social in another sense. Each person interacts with others who see things differently. To survive and prosper, each has to adjust to how other people see things. One has, in the light of experience, constantly to adjust to and to respond to others' perceptions and interpretations, and to anticipate their actions. They in turn respond, requiring yet further reorganizations of experience.

Third, in learning a language of the social group, one is alerted to certain features of the environment, rather than to others, for language is a kind of map of experience, a way of seeing, a way of making distinctions between different kinds of experience. By growing up into a social group, one is coming not only to experience things in a particular way, but also to acquire the tools for criticizing that way of experiencing and of transforming those experiences.

Therefore, the more one is left to oneself (cut off from social inter-action), the less progress will be made. One gets stuck. New ideas are not forthcoming. Furthermore, as Dewey argues, 'home education' is not sufficient to enable the child to anticipate the difficulties to be encountered in more complex social settings. A more purposeful reconstitution of experience is required.

Others can help and make suggestions – hence the importance of social groups in learning. Such a social group is formalized in the school to supplement the natural social groups of family or village. There the environment is extended; the social interactions enhanced. The school to some extent anticipates the problems to be tackled and offers the ideas that provide solutions – hence the delicate balance between pursuing an inquiry, coming across problems, seeking a solu-tion, on the one hand, and, on the other, being provided with possible answers from what is publicly known as the way forward. In this way one sees the 'answers', the 'given knowledge', to be rooted in inquiry and problem solving – not as pieces of knowledge disconnected from the struggle to understand and to act intelligently within the world. The role of the teacher must be seen in this light: selecting from the culture in order to get rid of the otherwise haphazard and possibly unfruitful stalemate in solving a problem, leading to frustration and boredom.

Therefore, there is a need for formal education, where the expe-riences of the social group are distilled and organized in some way with a view to aiding the development of experience of the young person. There simply is not the time or the opportunity for the child to undergo the growth of experience of the social group which has taken place over so many years. For example, how we come to expe-rience the world from a scientific point of view has emerged over a very long time. To have the concept of 'photosynthesis' changes the experience of gardening; it enables you to make connections that otherwise would not have been made; it changes what you can do, how you can anticipate events and how you might in turn trans-form the world with which you are interacting. Hence, teaching is the purposeful effort to enable the young person to shortcut this social development of experience through which one might be able to act upon and to transform the environment. 'Education, and education alone, spans the gap' between the lack of awareness of the young child and the accumulated modes of experiencing of the social group (DE, p. 3).

What education is not

One way of understanding a particular philosophical position is to see what it excludes – what other understandings of education, for instance, it is opposing. Especially in *Experience and Education*, Dewey disassociates himself from what he refers to as traditional and progressive educational movements, which at the time (1938) were respectively espoused by different protagonists in 'an arena of struggles practical and theoretical' (EE, p. 5). This is in answer to his critics, especially those who identified him with 'progressive ideas' or the 'new education', which, at the moment, I shall refer to as 'child-centered' notions of education. Indeed, Dewey, despite his protests, still remains associated with what are seen to be the evils of the child-centered education – hence the comments by Lord Joseph referred to on page 3.

Not 'traditional education'

Dewey first wishes to oppose what he refers to as 'traditional education' – a loose term, and one that purposely stereotypes a way of understanding education. But he is trying to pick out certain features of a dominant form of education – one that consists chiefly of the transmission of bodies of knowledge (information and skills), already conveniently organized into subjects, to a new generation. The connection between these transmitted bodies of knowledge and the prior experience of the learners may not exist, and that would not seem to matter. The irrelevance of that knowledge to experience, as perceived by the learner, is of no importance. The subject matter is intrinsically valuable. Its value does not lie in its being perceived as valuable by the learner.

Furthermore, such traditional learning would require the induction of the learner into a way of behaving that conforms to the standards of morality and manners which have also been inherited. No doubt that continuity of respectability would be reflected symbolically in all sorts of ways: school uniform, relationships of deference to the teacher, and so on. The teacher is the custodian of those bodies of knowledge and of those norms of behavior that are to be transmitted. He or she, therefore, is 'an authority', one whose judgment is to be respected. Indeed, ideally the qualification for being a teacher lies in the prior mastery of that body of knowledge and the commitment to certain principles of behaving. And the attitude of the student must be one of respect for this authority and submission to the truths that are contained within the knowledge transmitted (resulting in docility, passive receptivity and an overdose of book learning). The assessment of that knowledge as transmitted, and as learned by the student, would be seen as 'objective' in the sense that it appeals to standards of correctness which are non-negotiable. Furthermore, the most effective way of transmitting that knowledge and of inculcating those norms of good conduct is in a school, which is institutionally separated from ordinary experience (EE, p. 18).

It is important to understand what Dewey is and is not opposing, and to understand from what criticisms his own notion of educational aims is arising. Dewey is not opposing the significance of organized bodies of knowledge or their relevance to the educational growth of young people. On the other hand, nor is he *just* opposing the poor teaching that might often be associated with traditional education. He is opposing the disconnection very often of that learning from the significant experiences of the learners themselves. To this it may be objected that good teachers within the traditional fold often work hard to link it to the motives and interests of the young person. They strive, often successfully, to make the subject matter interesting. But the point that Dewey is making here is not that its educational value lies in its being made interesting or that appropriate motivating elements have previously been neglected. Rather, he is saying that the educational value of the subject matter lies in its logical connection with the experiences of the young person. There is a logical, not a contingent, connection between the two. This is fundamental to understanding Dewey and will be returned to again and again in this book – especially in Chapter 3, where we examine the concept of 'experience' in greater detail, and in Chapter 5, where we examine the notion of 'subject' and 'subject matter', and their relation to 'bodies of knowledge' and to inquiry.

For the moment, let us see the initial thrust of Dewey's criticism. He saw traditional forms of education, concerned as they were with the transmission of organized bodies of knowledge and with the grading of learners in terms of the successful or unsuccessful internalization of this knowledge, as becoming 'unduly formal or scholastic notions of education', which 'easily [become] remote and dead – abstract and bookish' (DE, p. 4). Traditional education gives the impression that knowledge is somehow 'completed', not itself open to change and development as a result of further inquiry and interpretation. There is the standing danger that the material of formal instruction will be merely the subject matter of the schools, isolated from the subject matter of life-experience, not necessarily connecting the meaning of a word or sentence or passage with experience or action.

However, it would be wrong to see Dewey as arguing simply against the bad teaching that might be associated with forms of traditional education. Behind the 'traditional learning' that he refers to is a *particular* philosophical understanding of 'liberal education', and it is his criticism of that which so incenses many of his critics. Dewey's account of traditional learning as summarized above may be a caricature of reality, but it does highlight features of a form of education that underlies many people's educational aims or educational criticisms. An ardent critic of Dewey, Anthony O'Hear, wrote strongly in defense of 'traditional learning' in the following terms: 'Education ... is irretrievably authoritarian and paternalistic ... imparting to a pupil something which he has yet to acquire ... The transmission is ... inevitably between unequals' (O'Hear, 1991, p. 5). Michael Oakeshott, in his defense of liberal education, says, 'In short, "school" is "monastic" in respect of being a place apart where excellence may be heard because the din of worldly laxities and partialities is silenced or abated' (1972, p. 69). Or, again, schools and universities 'are, then, sheltered places where excellences may be heard because the din of local partialities is no more than a distant rumble. They are places where a learner is initiated into what there is to be learnt' (Oakeshott, 1975, p. 24).

The account of liberal education given by Oakeshott, and by those who agree with him, is very different from that of Dewey. Put briefly, and therefore rather crudely, the one disconnects the learning to be cherished from everyday experiences (thus, the learner is 'initiated', in a place set apart); the other puts that 'din of local partialities' at the center of the educational experience. The metaphor of 'initiation' within that liberal tradition is a significant one, as is reflected in the title of Richard Peters' inaugural lecture at the University of London Institute of Education in 1967, because the young learner is seen to start from the outside of those forms of knowledge and experience through which he or she is to be liberated from ignorance. That requires an 'initiation' into a different form of experiencing. In similar vein in the USA, Bloom's influential book *Closing the American Mind* (1987) blamed a general state of ignorance, affecting policy and practice, upon the abandonment of traditional learning. The apparent contrast between these different understandings of education and its practice needs to be returned to later (see Chapters 6 and 8). Is the contrast irreconcilable? NO !

To sum up, Dewey's educational aims lie in the development of experience, as opposed to the acquisition of that knowledge and of those skills which do not connect with experience of the learner and which leave him or her untouched in any significant way – learned for the purposes of examinations, maybe, but not life-enhancing, not transforming how the learner thinks, feels or is disposed to act in a different way. That module on the environment, for example, in Year 10 geography is successfully completed and a good grade is obtained. But the young candidate still leaves all the lights on, fails to compost his or her waste and continues to pollute the atmosphere.

Not 'progressive education'

By contrast with what is depicted as 'traditional education', 'traditional standards' or 'traditional methods', many adopted what came to be referred to as 'progressive' educational approaches. Clearly, the account below, following Dewey, is, once again, a caricature; it puts into a few lines certain features that were and are more or less shared by a loose group of educational practices.

Roughly speaking, 'progressive education' saw perceived *relevance* to the interests and needs of the learner as central to education, not an element added by the good teacher to motivate the pupil to learn that which had no intrinsic interest for him or her. The interests and impulses of the young person would be the starting point of the education, not something attached to make the lessons more interesting. It was as though the authority of what should be learned had passed from the teacher to the learner, the teacher becoming a 'facilitator' of the child's learning. There is much talk about 'negotiation' of what should be learned and of its significance for the learner. The organization of knowledge into subjects may or may not be of value – it all depends on whether the learner finds it so, given the interests and concerns of the child. There is an intimate and necessary relation between the processes of actual experience and education (cf. EE, p. 20). The teacher would mediate, as it were, between that which was preserved in the organized bodies of knowledge and the problems and experiences of the young learner. The value of that mediation lay in the extent to which it modified the learner's outlook, attitude and skills, leading to yet further experiences and inquiries.

This is, of course, a caricature, for indeed the history of 'progressive education', with which Dewey was associated, but to which he was in some ways reacting, is and was complicated. One might distill this complexity, in the first decade of the twentieth century in the USA, into two connected but importantly different movements (see Cuban, 2004, pp. 45–7). On the one hand, there was a coalition of business, unions, universities and schools that called themselves 'progressives' in their criticism of a 'wasteful system of schooling' that was out of touch with society. Greater relevance was required to the needs of society and to the place of young people within it. There was a need for more vocational education, either within the common school or in 'industrial schools', as indeed was seen to be the case in Germany. Associated with this more vocationally oriented idea of progressivism was, too, the emphasis upon greater 'business-like efficiency', and indeed a greater use of testing to ensure appropriate learning experiences.

On the other hand, drawing upon the ideas of Dewey, others focused much more upon classroom practice and pedagogy, and

upon seeing the child as a whole (emotionally as well as intellectually). What others referred to as 'vocational relevance', these educational reformers described as 'learning by doing' – an emphasis
on practical intelligence and knowledge, which may or may not be
vocationally relevant. The educational value of what might be called
vocational lay not so much in its preparation for employment as in
its engagement of the interests and intellect of the young person.
Vocational, perhaps, but vocational in a much more generous sense
than it is frequently understood – as Dewey explained in Chapter 23
of *Democracy and Education*.

What these different versions of 'progressive education' had in
common was a certain skepticism about the over-reliance on subjects
and their transmission without the effort to see how their presenta-
tion might relate to the current interests and ways of conceiving the
world of the young people themselves. Boredom, far from being an
acceptable accompaniment of learning for so many, was seen by the
progressive educator as being the 'mortal sin' of education. But the
alternative was not to adopt the showbiz way of making the boring
lessons lively and interesting. It was to start with, and be guided by,
the interests themselves.

There are of course extreme examples of such a progressive
conception of education. In England in the 1960s there was the
much publicized account of William Tyndale School, where the
children were, under the banner of progressive and child-centered
approaches, allowed to select their own activities, unrestricted by
teachers (except in terms of safety and legal boundaries). The extensive review by the distinguished QC Mr Auld (The Auld Report, 1976)
was a turning point in the politics of education in England – a deter-
mination by government to return to more 'traditional standards'.

However, it would be wrong to ascribe such views to Dewey, as
some of his critics seem to do. Indeed, Dewey was himself highly
critical of those who, in endeavoring to reform a system that left so
many disengaged and untouched by the systematic transmission of
knowledge, overemphasized the centrality of the learners' impulses
and interests, and who focused on the problems of living in a changing
world such that past knowledge and wisdom were perceived to be
irrelevant. He was critical, too, of the abandonment by the teacher of

the role of authority in the shaping of the learning experience of the young person.

To understand Dewey one has to see what he was not – and he was neither a traditionalist nor a progressive as those are described above. And to understand what he was, one needs to attend more carefully to what he means by experience and how its transformation is central to educational practice. One example of what he could have meant is provided by a supporter and colleague, W.H. Kilpatrick, whose essay 'The project method' influenced generations of educationalists in both North America and Britain. This will be described in detail in Chapter 5. The child, actively inquiring, is disciplined by the activity rather than by external demands. The very language through which we understand the world is associated with our actions within that world or the effect that that world has upon us. Thus, to disconnect language (as in an education over-dependent on books) from the activity of the child is to make it alien, bereft of meaning, something that passively happens to one. But here we are into interesting and controversial understanding of 'meaning' – a philosophical position known as 'pragmatism', which we shall examine in greater depth in Part 3.

Not vocational training

The distinction is often made between academic education and vocational training, the former being identified with the acquisition of knowledge and understanding, the latter associated with the acquisition of skills useful for doing a job effectively. Students are directed up one or the other route – the one requiring the capacity to think and to theorize, the other the capacity to learn to perform particular tasks. Thus are perpetuated clear distinctions between different kinds of learner, educated or trained very often in different kinds of institution. The vocational activities take place in vocational institutions which are better resourced for the practical.

Certainly, Dewey distinguishes between educating and training. Animals can be trained, as can human beings. That means that they can develop habits and dispositions related to specific objects or kinds of objects. In so doing, they can be harnessed to the social purposes of human beings – the horse trained to plow, the dog trained to hunt. But, Dewey argues (DE, pp. 12–14), they cannot share in the social deliberations which put that training to particular uses. They cannot transcend the very specific goal-driven habituated behaviors they instinctively follow or are trained in. Put in a rather pompous way, they lack 'culture' – the acquired history of thinking and doing which enables them to cope differently with new experiences.

Of course human beings are trained. Habits of behavior are prompted. Humans can be made to respond to certain stimuli in predictable ways. But those responses shift with the responses of the group of which one is a potential member. One internalizes the understandings of the group, its emotions and its purposes. By acquiring their language, one is doing more than responding predictably to the stimuli or environment. These are interpreted, associated with other experiences, conceptualized in different ways. The habits remain useful for particular purposes, but the human being is transforming these habits into purposive actions which themselves are conceived as a result of mainly social interaction and experience.

Such purposive action, arising out of experiences and the reorganization of experience connected with it, distinguishes the educative process from mere training. Dewey wants to contrast the educated human being from one who is merely trained – to contrast a form of 'education', so called, that concentrates upon the formation of habits and with required responses to particular stimuli, with education, so called, because it transforms in some way how one experiences the world and is made capable of dealing with forthcoming experiences. What Dewey has in mind is the kind of schooling, prevalent in the USA then, as indeed it remains prevalent in Britain in many respects today, where precise targets are set and young people are trained to meet those targets – irrespective of whether the reaching of those targets affects them personally, deep down. Somehow they remain much the same after the experience or the gaining of the new skill or habit.

In arguing this, Dewey is right to contrast the *concepts* of education and training. To train is to train to do X – something quite specific. There is no necessary implication that there is any growth of knowledge or understanding – indeed, any conscious recognition of the skill or habit acquired. Furthermore, there is no implication that what is achieved is valuable. The trained pickpocket, though highly skilled, is not engaged in an activity that is regarded as worthwhile. 'Education', by contrast, implies much more than that. It implies that there is a development of understanding. It implies that relevant concepts have been acquired and that one is experiencing the world in a different, more sophisticated way. Furthermore, there is the implication that, in certain resects, that different way of seeing things is an improvement. Education indicates improvement, a more comprehensive and deeper way of seeing things.

However, although the *concepts* of education and training might be contrasted (that is, they are not to be treated synonymously), one and the same activity might be both training and educational. One can be trained to use a chisel in the sense of acquiring a particular habit; that habit, having been acquired, could, in appropriate circumstances, be exercised with relatively little thought and reflection. It remains precisely that – a habit. But habits can be reflected upon. They can be changed and adapted as circumstances demand. They become part of a wider scheme of thought, a purposive agenda informed by conscious aims and purposes. Hence, the carpenter can be trained in an educational environment, seeing his or her new-found skill (into which he or she has been habitualized) within a wider critical appraisal of the purposes that the skill or habit is intended to serve. There is a difference between the skilled painter and the educated one who is able to utilize the habits of his or her training to create something new and imaginative. Such a painter is more than trained, but the training is an essential tool for that transformation of experience. It is an extension of the capacity to experience. Although the difference might be characterized by the difference between outward and inward modification of the learner, the contrast cannot be too sharp, as Dewey argues (DE, p. 11), because the external modification changes the interaction that the learner has with the objects of the world; it affects the very experience of it. The training in this or that habit or skill, therefore, is part of the educational process.

This point is made effectively and at some length in Chapter 23 of *Democracy and Education*, entitled 'Vocational aspects of education'. Dewey argues for a broad definition of 'vocation':

A vocation means nothing but such a direction of life activities as renders them perceptibly significant to a person, because of the consequences they accomplish, and also useful to his associates. The opposite of a career is neither leisure nor culture, but aimlessness, capriciousness, the absence of cumulative achievement in experience, on the personal side, and idle display, parasitic dependence upon the others, on the social side.

(DE, p. 307)

Furthermore, 'occupation is a concrete term for continuity': the linking of experiences through some activity, whether it be painting, running a business, studying science.

Dewey, then, is arguing against the bewitchment of simple dualisms – those between education and training, between leisure activities and occupation or job, between academic and vocational. Growth – that constant transformation of experience and the development of capacities to deal with further experiences – takes place in many places and through different demands. Activities of different kinds, occupations and relationships interact, each with the other, as part of living. Each has a part in the transformation of experiences and thus of the person's growing capacity to adapt to new situations. Life should be seen as a whole, not as fragmented into discrete bits and pieces. As Dewey continues to argue, each person has a number of callings: earning a living, supporting a family, coming to the assistance of others, enjoying the company of friends. Each of these interacts with, and transforms, the experience of each of the others. The educative process, as opposed to a mere training in a specific skill (let us say as a lathe operator), recognizes and encourages this broader interaction. The preparation to be a lathe operator, therefore, would enable the operator to see his or her skilled performance within a broader personal and social context.

Not a means to some other end

A recent report in England showed the problems which young people now have in managing their personal finances: getting into unpayable debt, spending beyond their means and failing to put money aside for their pensions. The Secretary of State for Education and Skills for England responded by saying that personal financial management must be introduced to the curriculum. It was in response to this kind of role bestowed on education that Dewey responded in 1916: 'The public school is the willing packhorse of our social system; it is the true hero of the refrain: let George do it' (quoted in Cuban, 2004).

It is so easy to see 'education', in its descriptive sense, as a means to achieve some end that is only contingently connected with the very idea of education, and thus constantly to ask schools to do whatever is seen to be necessary to reach some further social and government target, such as fewer pregnancies among teenagers or a greater proportion of students achieving high scores in tests. But should education be seen in this way? Certainly, the view that it should is something which Dewey challenges.

The distinction needs to be explained. If I catch a bus in order to get to the bank before it closes, the former (catching the bus) is a means to achieving a particular end or goal (getting to the bank on time), but the relation of the one to the other is purely contingent. There is no intrinsic or conceptual or logical relation between the two. I could equally have caught a taxi or driven there in my car. The meaning of being at the bank on time is in no way affected by the means of transport.

But take another example. The parent teaches the child to say 'please' as one means, among many, of forming his character as a polite person. The one is a means to the overall goal of moral formation. But the relationship is not a merely contingent one. Being polite means adopting a certain attitude toward other people, and such an attitude is embodied in the social usage of words such as 'please' and 'thank you'.

Or take the example of the teacher teaching simultaneous equations. The reason is that to do so is a means of teaching algebra, and teaching algebra is a means of teaching mathematics, and teaching mathematics is a means of educating the young person. But in each case, the means of attaining the specific end is not contingently related to that end (understanding algebra, thinking mathematically, being an educated person). Rather, it is part of what we mean by the end. We teach mathematics because being able to think mathematically is part of what we mean by an 'educated person'. And the idea of an educated person is not a means to anything. Rather, it is a form of being that is thought to be worthwhile in itself, not as a means to something else.

Of course, those activities that are part of the *educational* experience might also be useful for some non-educational purpose such as being successful at business – or, indeed, in helping the young person sort out his or her personal finances. But that is not what makes them educational. Indeed, such activities are almost sure to fail, since they are stuck on, as it were, to an enterprise without their having any relationship to the wider understanding of experience or to the wider moral formation. What makes an experience educational is its transformational character – the way in which it makes one think and therefore experience differently. It is not educational because, without having any significant transformational power, it offers a useful tool for achieving some other end.

This 'integration' of the ends of an activity with the means by which those ends are attained is crucial to an understanding of Dewey's concept of education and of its connection to a deeper philosophical analysis of a 'practice'. Dewey, in *Democracy and Education*, Chapter 8, criticized those who wanted to 'set up' ends 'from without' (he would have been vitriolic had he foreseen the target setting that presently goes on). In so doing, he distinguished between the 'results', the 'ends', the 'ends-in-view' and the 'aims' of an action. The results of an action are events consequential upon it and causally explicable by it. An 'end', however, is more than a result; it 'terminates and completes' the action, and leads to another. Thus, the bee's 'making of wax' terminates the gathering of pollen and leads to the building of cells – each action being 'intrinsically continuous with what precedes'. To have an 'end-in-view', however, is to be conscious of what completes the present ongoing action – to see its natural termination. Finally, to have an aim is to act intelligently in the light of the 'end-in-view' – that is, to act purposefully in the light of current circumstances. Dewey, therefore, is critical of the notion (implicit within the means–end model that is espoused by educational planners) that an end is something that can be defined and comprehended in isolation from the activities by which it is attained. Furthermore, he maintains that even if it could be so identified and isolated, one could not then adopt means to attain it while the end (to be attained) remains the same, as though an activity is commenced and completed in a vacuum. In particular, this would be logically and morally reprehensible in teaching – logically, because it ignores the logical point that an activity by the pupil must be identified in the pupil's terms if it is to be the pupil's activity; morally, because it does not respect the ongoing interests and activities that are valued by the pupil.

The crux of Dewey's argument, therefore, is that a logical separation is made between 'means' and 'ends' when they are 'intrinsically continuous'. The upshot of this false distinction would be that it fails to do justice to the continual adjustment to circumstances that typifies most action; in any ongoing situations, how one conceives what one is doing at the moment enters into how one conceives the possible outcome. Furthermore, the more observant one is of the present circumstances – the more alternatives one sees as possible outcomes – the more connections one will see the 'end-in-view' to have with other events. 'Intelligent action', therefore, is the constant adaptation to circumstances, and the reformulation of goals in the light of this adaptation. Such intelligent action cannot be understood in terms of logically discrete 'means' causing a preconceived 'end': the means is transformed by the end-in-view, and the end-in-view is constantly being transformed by the circumstances through which the 'means' is trying to attain it – the means themselves constantly changing as one reflects on the process. The danger, according to Dewey, is yet again not to see connections – to make clear distinctions where things need to be seen as a whole. Moreover, as one is approaching the evolving ends-in-view, the attempts or activities one is engaged in will embody further principles that shape the purposive activity.

There will be, in other words, 'aims' which are embodied in the very 'striving for the end-in-view' and which will transform that striving. At no stage can one say 'mission accomplished', because what previously had been an 'end-in-view' has now become a stage in some further activity. Teaching as a practice is not a means to an end. It is this realizing of an end-in-view, which itself is being transformed in the attempt to realize it. That attempt to realize it is transformed by the

interaction with the learners (with their understandings and motivations), and it is transformed, too, by the teacher's growing understanding of the subject matter as it is put before the learner.

Education, therefore, is this constant transformation of experience
as one seeks some end-in-view, which initially may be seen as though
through a glass darkly. Anyone who has tried to write will know what
I mean. The purpose of the writing, the 'end-in-view', is only dimly
perceived to begin with, but is gradually shaped and made more
definite in its pursuit, and the end product may well be different
from the end-in-view as perceived at the beginning As one seeks to
solve a problem, as one engages in an inquiry and as one reflects upon
the various means and circumstances in which that inquiry is taking
place, so the very inquiry is transformed, and gives rise to further
problems and further inquiries.

That is why the aim of education is seen to be one of constant
'growth'.

Education as growth

It is apparent from the above that Dewey's educational aims were
logically tied to his understanding of persons as in a state of constant
change, which results from their experiences and from the material
and social conditions in which they live and have to survive. In that
sense, they were like any living organism. The plants in the allotment,
though having certain 'impulses' to get larger, to have leaves, to ger-
minate and to fruit, are constantly having to adapt to circumstances
such as changes in weather or in soil conditions. They grow in that
they fulfill their potential as cabbages or runner beans, but if they do
not have the appropriate conditions with which to interact, growth
will cease and they will die.

Dewey constantly talks of the learner as a living organism which,
to survive, needs to adapt to changing circumstances. But he sees the
limitations of the purely biological metaphor. That interaction is not
so much one of a biological organism interacting with another, but
of a social being interacting with other social beings and with the
artifacts and institutions on which other human beings have left their

mark. That interaction can also be with the 'accumulated wisdom of the race' if that is made accessible to the living, experiencing, problem-solving 'organism'.

Hence, no human being stays the same. Every experience makes its mark – reinforcing a way of seeing things, challenging previous conceptions or opening up new possibilities ('ends-in-view'). This is what constitutes 'growth' – the 'cumulative movement of action towards a later result' (DE, p. 41). How one sees things at any one moment has arisen from a prior way of seeing things and has, if only minimally, transformed that way. The activity (the movement) is itself to be understood in terms of the accumulation of experiences, and does itself result in yet further 'accumulation'. Ideally, that transformation enables the person to deal more effectively with new experiences or makes possible courses of action that previously were not known or that seemed too difficult to embark upon. Growth, therefore, indicates not only change but increase or improvement in quality. And that quality, minimally, refers to the increased capacity to have further experiences and to deal with problems that have arisen through the prior experiences. Dewey explains that he is referring to

> the ability to learn from experience; the power to retain from one experience something which is of avail in coping with the difficulties of a later situation. This means power to modify actions on the basis of the results of prior experiences, the power to develop dispositions. Without it, the acquisition of habits is impossible.
>
> (DE, p. 44)

The development of habits is crucial to this growth – the internalization of a way to respond to further experiences. Such internalization arises from the success with which certain behaviors or actions have enabled one to cope with experience. But such habits (of thinking as well as of behaving) must not become 'habituations' – that is, so fixed that they cannot adapt to very new circumstances. Habits, though themselves the tools of growth, need to be sharpened, made flexible, subject to critical scrutiny lest they prevent adaptation and get in the way of problem solving. Rigid habits can stunt growth rather than enhance it.

Growth, therefore, is an evaluative, not just a descriptive, concept. It marks the increased capacity for experiencing and for having further experiences – the very conditions of living as a human, social being.

The influence of those who have emphasized 'growth' as an educational aim is reflected in several policy documents in Britain. The 1932 Hadow Report on primary education in England and Wales stated:

> In framing the curriculum for the primary school . . . our main care must be to supply children between the ages of seven and eleven with what is essential to their healthy growth – physical, intellectual and moral – during that particular stage of their development. The principle which is here implied will be challenged by no one who has grasped the idea that life is a process of growth in which there are successive stages, each with its own successive stages and needs.
>
> (Hadow Report, 1932, p. 92)

The Plowden Report of 1967, *Children and Their Primary Schools*, provided in its first chapter a theoretical and philosophical overview of the detailed recommendations it was to make. It is as though the ghost of Dewey were standing beside Lady Plowden as she wrote it, and his influence is recognized by Brian Simon in his historical account of the report (1991, p. 362). The report spoke of the one characteristic that all children have in common: 'a strong drive' from a very early age 'towards activity in the exploration of the environment', linked to the child's 'curiosity, especially about novel and unexpected features of his experience' (para. 45). 'Development' is interpreted as the result of the 'complex and continuous interaction between the developing organism and its environment' (para. 11).

There, of course, lies the difficulty, as the critics of the Plowden Report were quick to point out. The assumption is that one can read off, as it were, what counts as growth in this evaluative sense from attending to the nature or essence of the object growing. Just as we can distinguish between the growth of a plant and its decay or the stunting of its growth (between what is proper to the plant and what is not), so too can we distinguish between the growth of a person and the stunting of that growth, and do so simply in terms of the essence of what it is to be a growing, social being whose very essence is to interact with other social beings, and thus constantly to transform existing experiences in a way that makes them even more fruitful, more problem-solving. Growth in this sense becomes an end in itself. But, the critics would argue: can one not distinguish between healthy and unhealthy growth? Does not the evaluation of educational growth lie not simply in the nature of growth itself, but in what that growth leads to? The criteria of educational growth cannot be internal to what we mean by growth. This controversial ethical dimension will be postponed to Chapter 6. More needs to be said, first, about the nature of experience itself, about the nature of the interests of the learner which are to be developed and about the way in which some interests, and not others, are to be directed if there is to be genuine growth.

of ch 6

Meanwhile, the purpose of school education is to ensure the continuance of education by organizing the powers that ensure growth (DE, p. 54). The school is a continuance and an enhancement of social life, where, because of the complexity of that social life, a more focused attempt is required to ensure the appropriate experiences – experiences that will empower the person to have a more fruitful experiencing of the physical and social worlds he or she inhabits.

Conclusion: the aims of education revisited

To ask for the aim of education is not to ask for an end that is clearly defined and that can be reached so long as certain learning activities are pursued. The aim is not an end separate from the means of its accomplishment. Rather, to state the aim of education is to spell out the values that permeate or are embodied in those learning activities. How should one characterize the learning that we judge to be educational?

To answer that question, Dewey attends to the nature of the learner. The learner is a living, social organism, who lives by constant adaptation to the conditions – material and social – in which he or she

nothing more?

survives. A significant part of that adapting lies in the reconceptualizing of the circumstances in which one is living, and of the 'ends-in-
view' of one's activities, in the light of experience. Such a reconceptualizing has no end; it is part of what it means to live.

The social conditions in which one is living also contain the accumulated wisdom of past generations. This accumulated wisdom – the
result of other people's experiences and interactions with others –
does itself provide a powerful set of experiences which empower the
learner all the more. But they have to be linked with the experiences,
not nearly so refined and sophisticated, of the learner. There lies the
art and skill of the teacher.

As that transformation takes place through exposure to others'
narratives and to the critical conversations of others in the school
and elsewhere, so the unity, continuity and interaction of experiences themselves become a challenge. Otherwise, the experiences
remain hermetically sealed off from each other, and that impoverishes each set of experiences (as when the experiences of doing science are sealed off from the experiences of religion). Hence, living
itself requires the constant transformation of experience – the shift
from immaturity (defined in terms of having a limited set and organization of experience, thereby being ill-prepared to meet many of the
situations that arise), to ever-increasing maturity. But so long as there
is life, and interaction with the material and social environment, so
that maturing will never stop. Growth has no end other than further
growth.

Therefore, education so conceived is incompatible with, first, the
simple transmission of 'knowledge' that does not connect up with
the young person's experience; second, the undirected experiences
which might do little to enhance the capacity or the propensity for
more experience; third, the disconnection of learning from the lived
and motivating experiences of the learner – the interests that demand
intelligent responses, the inquiries that require the reconceptualizing
of understandings of situations or problems encountered. Where one
sees this constant transformation taking place, where experiences
challenge old conceptions, where old experiences give rise to more
powerful ways of inquiring and problem solving, there is growth, and
it requires no justification beyond itself. That is the aim of education.

Dewey sums it up as follows:

Our net conclusion is that life is development, and that developing, growing, is life. Translated into its educational equivalent, that means: (i) that the educational process has no end beyond itself; and that (ii) the educational process is one of continual reorganizing, reconstructing, transforming ... The purpose of school education is to insure the continuance of education by organizing the powers that insure growth. The inclination to learn from life itself and to make the conditions of life such that all will learn in the process of living is the finest product of schooling.

(DE, pp. 50, 51)

There are difficulties that have been raised and that need to be explored further. One such difficulty, already mentioned, lies in the idea of growth as an end in itself, irrespective of the further experiences or ends-in-view that it gives rise to. Second, the concept of 'experience' is being asked to do an awful lot of work. To that we must turn in the next chapter. The ethical problems of growth as an end in itself will be postponed to Chapter 6.

Chapter 3

Experiencing, Making Sense, Knowing and Inquiring

Experience: a key concept

Chapter 2 of *Experience and Education* is entitled 'The need of a theory of experience'. That need arises from Dewey's empiricism, namely the belief that all knowledge and understanding ultimately derive from experience and must in some way or another relate back logically to experience. Indeed, if one needed one hook on which to hang Dewey's philosophy of education, it would be that of 'experience' and its enrichment – hence the title of his book published in 1938 to explain as briefly as possible to skeptics and critics what the central ideas of his educational philosophy were. In *Democracy and Education* he refers to 'a new philosophy of experience and knowledge' (p. 273).

One reason why Dewey made 'experience' a focus of his writings was the lack of importance attached to 'experience' in the dismal experience of education itself suffered by young learners. As Dewey expounds in Chapter 20 of *Democracy and Education*, 'experience' is too often seen as something different from and inferior to knowledge; it is identified with being practical and with the *particular* circumstance, thereby lacking (as far as 'traditionalists' were concerned) the superior theoretical understanding that is what education seeks to impart. As a result, in the practice of education, that theory would be transmitted mainly to those with superior intelligence, without recourse to experience; only to those who are very weak at theory would there be given a more experience-based learning program. While those who are strong in intelligence would be learning scientific theory, those who are intellectually feeble would be doing practical, applied or experiential science such as growing things (rural science) or making things for the home (domestic science). And, indeed, that attitude still prevails. In England there are plans to remove much of the practical coursework from A level geography to make more room for the theory that needs to be transmitted. 'Fieldwork', once seen as an essential component of geographical studies, is being relegated to a minor role.

However, as Dewey argues, 'An ounce of experience is better than a ton of theory because it is only in experience that any theory has vital and verifiable significance (DE, p. 144). Otherwise, without experience, one has but 'verbal formulae' and the logical relations between such formulas – a mental game disconnected from the purposive activity they are meant to serve. And thus, for Dewey, experience came to mean 'the apprehension of material which should ballast and check the exercise of reasoning' (DE, p. 267).

The second, connected reason why Dewey focused upon the importance of experience in education lay in the central place that experience (as he came to define it) had in his theory of knowledge and thus in his theory of the development of knowledge through education. The distinction between thinking and experiencing, and thus between knowledge (the product of thinking) and experience, was one of the 'false dualisms' which distorts educational programs and against which Dewey so strenuously fought.

Philosophical background

In so fighting, Dewey took on what he saw to be two rival philosophical positions: that of rationalism on the one hand and that of classical empiricism on the other. The first of these two would seem, in Dewey's account, to owe the errors of its ways to Plato – but was enshrined within a 'rationalist tradition' reflected, as all philosophy undergraduates would have learned, in Descartes, Leibniz and Spinoza.

The statement of Plato that philosophers should be kings may best be understood as a statement that rational intelligence, and not habit, appetite, impulse and emotion, should regulate human

affairs. The first of these secures order, unity, and law; the others signify multiplicity and discord, irrational fluctuations from one estate
to another.

(DE, p. 263)

Plato's 'real world' was the world of ideas, of which the world of
experience was but a poor shadow. The world of experience was transient, ephemeral, distorted by emotion. The person who depended
on experience would be like the person described in *The Republic*,
who, entrapped within the cave, could see only shadows of the imitation of the real world on the back of the cave.

The rival position was that of classical empiricism, where 'the real'
was the set of experiences that one received. These experiences
impressed themselves upon the mind. They were the foundations,
which were built on through an association of one experience with
another in order to establish correlations, and thereby predictions of
further experiences in similar circumstances. Again, the subject, the
person, the learner would be one who observes, in this case not the
world of ideas but the experiences that passed before his or her gaze.

In one way, knowledge as something that is built upon a foundation
of experience seems sensible enough. Knowledge, so the argument
would run, starts with observation of the world as experienced and
then, through the process of induction, arrives at general propositions
about what has been observed. Those general propositions are then
checked against further experience. If they are not confirmed by
further observation of experience, then they need to be adjusted. If
we had never seen, heard, felt, tasted or smelled anything at all, we
would not have any thoughts or anything to think about.

But the history of empiricism as a philosophical position is much
more complicated than such an obvious statement would imply. First,
what do we directly experience? Is what I see before me a patch of
color of a certain shape or is it a pullover? Does what I see or hear
leave a direct impression on my 'mind' (as on a *tabula rasa* or on an
otherwise 'clean slate') or is it affected either by previous impressions
or, indeed, by the active interpretation of the receiving mind? Indeed,
is there a 'mind', distinguishable from the physical world, upon which
that physical world leaves its impressions, either uninterpreted by the

mind (which is but a collection of such impressions) or reconstructed by the mind?

The history of empiricism is one, first, of varying interpretations of what *is* the object of experience, and, second, of the role of 'mind' in receiving and forming that experience. Professor A.J. Ayer (1947–8) attempted to reduce all knowledge to a construction from sense data, which, in the ultimate analysis, are the objects of experience; what I see is a maroon patch of a certain shape, not a pullover. The pullover is a complex summary of different experiences, and a kind of hypothesis, inducted from experience, that these different sensations will cling together in a certain way.

The major problem that Dewey had with both the rationalist and the empiricist traditions was the dualism between the 'object known' and the 'subject knowing', and thus with the 'spectator' metaphor of knowing – that is, with the notion of the mind as something that views and thinks about what is observed, whether that be the world of ideas or the world of sensations, sense data or emotions.

Not to have a 'theory of experience' would be to ignore these philosophical questions, which have a profound implication for education. And yet any theory or practice of education must have a place for 'experience', however that is understood. Learning does depend upon experiencing something, even if it is only the dictated lecture notes of the teacher. But the kind of experience the learner is exposed to presupposes, albeit rarely recognized or made explicit, an underlying view of what is the object of experience, what it means to experience that object and what would count as experiencing that something significantly. The teacher, dictating notes, is assuming that the experience of hearing these notes is the basis of understanding and knowledge, and that some valuable learning is taking place. But the experience of the learner might be the tone of voice, the sounds which make no sense, the surrounding atmosphere of disengagement – sensations upon which little is built by way of knowledge. Indeed, they may be the very sensations, imbued with certain emotions, that put the learner off the pursuit of knowledge or deaden the brain. Or it may be that these sounds impress themselves 'upon the mind' to the extent that they can be repeated at the appropriate stimulus.

One understanding of experience, contemporaneous with Dewey, which quite explicitly shaped what it meant to learn and which influenced classroom practice for decades to come, was that of the 'stimulus–response' school of behaviorist psychologists associated with J.B. Watson, who was a graduate student at Chicago during Dewey's period there (see Ryan, 1995, pp. 124–5). This brand of behaviorism dispensed with 'the mind'. We are really no more than physical objects, the behavior of which can be causally explained, as is the case with all physical objects. Our behavior is but a response to certain stimuli, and one can work out 'the laws' whereby a particular stimulus would 'cause' a particular response, given the appropriate conditions. Specific physical 'rewards' (e.g. the availability of food) would stimulate specific behaviors. Specific 'punishments' (e.g. the imposition of pain) would stimulate or cause aversive behavior. The gradual withdrawal of rewards or punishments would weaken the causal link between stimulus and response.

Seeing where Dewey stood in relation to his contemporary's account of learning helps us to understand what Dewey meant by experience. First, Watson got rid of 'the mind' as a separate substance, distinct from the body. The problem of 'the ghost in the machine' was solved by the exorcism of the ghost. The dualism of 'mind' and 'body', no doubt always hovering in the background of philosophy but dominant since Descartes, was one of the dualisms that Dewey sought to dissolve. In that sense, Dewey was a behaviorist. There is continuity between humankind and nature – between the ways in which animals learn behaviorally and the learning of the higher animals, namely humankind. Such continuity was denied by the dualistic philosophy that Dewey argued against, which set mental agency apart from the material world in which that agency had to operate. As he argued, 'This philosophy is vouched for by the doctrine of biological development which shows that man is continuous with nature, not an alien entering her processes from without' (DE, p. 285).

However, Dewey was critical of the 'behaviorism' of Watson and his colleagues for the following reason. The stimulus does not impact on a purely passive object. Nor does it shape that object in its response, as though previous stimuli had not affected the way in which the stimulus was to be received. Rather, the object 'being stimulated' is an organism, which not only reacts to a stimulus but adapts it to its own previous tendencies and ways of behaving. The stimulus, in other words, is 'interpreted' (a mentalistic term that Dewey did not seem able to dispense with).

If, therefore, experience, in this dissolution of the mind–body dualism, was neither the idea, which one had in one's head, nor the feeling, sensation or whatever, which one had through the body, what could it be?

Having an experience

Not only does the experiencing organism assimilate previous experiences, thereby both adapting to them and affecting the nature of further experiences, but there is also a teleological aspect to the responding. The adaptation of the organism to the stimulus is purposive, usually for the survival and greater good of the organism. The plant responds to the stimulus of the Sun with a view to its nourishment and growth; where there is lack of water, its roots go deeper, with a view to finding sustenance. Similarly, children will build into their responsive system ways of behaving that are conducive to survival and well-being – as when, following a painful stimulus, they will adapt their behavior to the experience of a flame or fire:

> It is not experience when a child merely sticks his finger into a flame; it is experience when the movement is connected with the pain which he undergoes in consequence. Henceforth, the sticking of the finger into flames means a burn.
>
> (DE, p. 139)

There is, then, both an active and a passive element in experience: a trying (or experimenting) and an undergoing (or consequence). This 'undergoing' affects the next 'trying'. The consequences of one's 'trying', as it were, enter into how we experience things in the future; it attaches significances to the next 'trying'. Experience, then, is part of action, and it both flows into the active organism and is transformed by the activity itself, as the organism reacts purposively to the next situation. An experience, therefore, is 'interpreted' by the adaptations that have occurred in previous experiencing. There is, in that sense, a cognitive element in an experience; experience is not something that, uninterpreted, imposes itself upon the passive mind.

Moreover, that experience takes place in activities that have an 'end in view'. The organism is active. It is engaged in purposive behavior. The experience, therefore, is seen, or given significance, in the light of these 'ends-in-view' and will in turn affect them. That may appear at first to put Dewey's account at odds with the biological and evolutionary continuity between lower and higher levels of organisms, since the 'ends-in-view' that enter into the account of human activity would appear to be different in kind from the adaptive behavior of plants and animals. But that is not so, as Dewey points out in *Experience and Nature*:

> Plants and non-human animals act *as if* they were concerned that their activity . . . should maintain itself. Even atoms and molecules show a selective bias in their indifferences, affinities and repulsions when exposed to other events. With respect to some things they are hungry to the point of greediness; in the presence of others they are sluggish and cold. It is not surprising that naïve science imputed appetition . . . to all natural processes . . . In a genuine, although not psychic sense, natural beings exhibit preferences and centeredness.
>
> (EN, p. 208)

The value of the experience, therefore, lies in the connections it leads to – the fruitfulness of the adaptations that take place as a result. Thus, the child who burns his finger in the candle flame will perceive that flame differently in future; he will respond differently to further acquaintance with it; it will have a different meaning; the experience of fresh acquaintance with a flame will embody the accumulation of previous experiences and will flow into different ways of behaving.

Hence, for Dewey there is an evolutionary continuity between the simple organisms of plants and the much more complex ones of human being. This evolutionary continuity is the inevitable result of Dewey's ridding himself of the dualism of mind and body. With such a biological model in mind, Dewey saw the young learner as being ever in a state of adapting to new stimuli, the adapted organism reacting thereby differently to the next lot of stimuli, and so on. The stimulus has a particular 'meaning' as a result of previous stimuli and of the adaptations that have taken place to accommodate them. Therefore, the same stimulus will not be responded to in exactly the same way by different human organisms, because each organism will have adapted somewhat differently to prior stimuli and hence will 'interpret' the new one in a somewhat different way.

No doubt certain stimuli (potential experiences) are ignored. They do not connect with the interpretive systems (that is, the connections already internalized) of the organism. The organism is absorbed with other tendencies and inclinations. Or the stimuli are too complex to be adapted to. For stimuli to have an effect, they have, in some way or other, to fit into the current mode of interpreting and thus into the active search for meaning.

Such a view needs to be contrasted with its alternative, namely the separation of mind (the subject doing the experiencing) and the body (where the experience takes place). Dewey says of this that 'the intimate union of activity and undergoing its consequences which leads to recognition of meaning is broken; instead we have two fragments: mere bodily action on one side, and meaning directly grasped by "spiritual" activity on the other' (DE, p. 140).

In the non-dualistic 'theory of experience' that Dewey argues for, the senses are the 'avenues of knowledge'. The knowledge of the kite flyer, for example, is *in the hands*, as the person (the organism) responds to various forces and adjusts technique, incorporating what has been 'learned' into fresh manipulations of the kite. This experience of kite flying develops, as it incorporates the 'know-how' gained from previous experience and as it anticipates fresh experience as a result (see DE, p. 142). A very young child will play with a simple toy or a piece of newspaper, 'testing out' what can be done with it, incorporating its achievement into its subsequent play, extending its operations on the object, opening up further possibilities to be explored. There is no thinking separate from the doing, and yet the child – the living and purposefully active organism – is extending its repertoire of habit and skill and its control of the environment.

It is necessary to pause a little to see the educational implications of this 'theory of experience' – of this essential unity of mind and body in the purposeful activity of an organism.

First, it makes sense of what many teachers implicitly believe, namely that one thinks in some sense with the body – the artist and craftsman with the hands, the dancer with the whole body, the football (soccer) player with the feet, the chef with the trial and error of preparing a meal, the young mother with handling the baby. There are not two actions: that of the mind thinking and that of the body carrying out instructions from the mind – often later and in a different setting. Rather, the experiences of painting, dancing, playing football, cooking and mothering embody the consequence of previous experience and anticipates how further experiences will be internalized. Experience is both a way of understanding or interpreting what happens and a way of anticipating what happens in the future or what to do next. There is both a cognitive and a conative element. Its very structure screens out other possible experiences and renders other possible ones more accessible.

Second, this 'theory of experience' attaches supreme importance to 'doing' and 'making' as a way of knowing. That is, the experiencing in purposeful activity is a way of understanding. The teacher, through a wide range of experience, which is constantly adapted to reach certain ends-in-view, will have a different kind of knowledge from the person who has simply read about teaching in books. Despite the attempt to make of teaching a 'science' (see Reynolds, 1998), teaching is a 'doing', a purposive activity with 'ends-in-view', namely that the learner should come to see things in a different, better-informed way. Furthermore, intelligent teaching is not a matter of applying theory or research to the act of teaching; it is a matter of adapting appropriately to different circumstances – to have learned from previous experiences, even if that learning cannot be articulated. And in so doing, the teacher will be making possible the kinds of experiences that fit with the present way of the learners' experiencing and also challenge and extend it. (This point will be developed at length in Chapter 4, which focuses upon the education of the learners' 'interests'.)

Third, what Dewey is saying reinforces the importance attached to habit and to skill. Habit is the way in which the organism has come to deal, without hesitation, with certain circumstances and problems. The habit incorporates ways of reacting that have been acquired and reinforced through successful experiences, and as such they are the shapers of further experiences. They thus empower the learner in his or her further explorations and the development of further, more complex habits. Of course, such habits might be inappropriate for new situations. Habits may need, in new circumstances, to be broken or transformed, but without them the young learner would be unable to deal with the multitude of experiences that he or she faces. Furthermore, the way of dealing with these experiences, even habitually, depends on varying degrees of skill – the acquired ability to coordinate bodily powers appropriately and habitually to bring about new situations. Such skills and habits extend the powers of the person. They free the person from effort so that more thought can be given to further problems or ends-in-view.

Fourth, the intelligent 'doing' is acquired through 'doing', though no doubt assisted by the corrections from an experienced other. 'Intelligent doing' is not learned from lectures on 'doing' or from the transmission of theory about 'doing'. The apprenticed engineer or hairdresser learns from tackling practical problems, albeit guided and corrected by an experienced mentor. The knowledge acquired from previous problems tackled (that is, the organization of previous experiences with a view to meeting new circumstances and problems) 'flows into' the subsequent problem solving. Education should therefore be largely practical, active, engaged with problems.

Interpretation, knowledge and meaning

I have just defined 'knowledge' as 'the organization of previous experiences with a view to meeting new circumstances'. That does not presuppose a conscious organization of that experience. It is internal to the organism's purposeful activity. Each experience is an interpretation of new circumstances, that interpretation itself evolving in the need to adapt to and accommodate the new circumstances.

However, such organization of experience (such practical knowledge) can be reflected upon. It can be, and is, formulated into propositions – although such propositional knowledge could never capture completely the experiential knowledge that informs action.

Furthermore, that propositional knowledge, arising from a reflection on, and a formulation of, experience, needs to be related back to experience. It lacks validity where it has been disconnected from the experience from which it arises and of which it is supposed to make sense. Disconnected from experience, such 'knowledge' is but a world of formulas and ideas without attachment to the world of experience from which it arose and which it is supposed to represent.

An example of such a separation would be in the teaching of mathematics, where the formulas are learned as such, disconnected from activities to which they are relevant and disconnected from the world, in which the experiencing of things in terms of quantified relationships affects further experiencing. Such 'experience' has no meaning. Connections are not made. The person remains much as before, uninfluenced by what is happening. The so-called learning is purely mechanical, and, as Dewey argues, 'Any way is mechanical which narrows down the bodily activity so that a separation of body from mind – that is, from recognition of meaning – is set up' (DE, p. 143).

But what is this active search for meaning? To understand that, one must grasp the significance of 'having a problem' and the subsequent 'inquiry'.

The organism adapts because its normal activity is in some way arrested. It is prevented from doing what it has been programmed to do. This is the case with the lowest and simplest forms of organism, but how much more is it the case with human beings. A person is prevented from proceeding in the normal way. That creates a problem. Various solutions are sought; different responses tried out. When a response 'works' (that is, when the problem is removed), then that person adapts accordingly. A new way of responding has been acquired and internalized, thus providing the future capacity to handle similar problems. A 'problem' leads to the search for a 'solution', which then leads to 'growth' – that is, a more complex interpretive system that increases the capacity to deal with further experiences. Having a problem sets one going, and in answering the problem one comes across further problems, and so on. This gives greater, but not unlimited, control (more problems will arise in the exercise of that control) over the self and the environment. In this way, progress and growth are ensured.

In *How We Think*, Dewey sees problems to be 'forked road' situations (HWT, pp. 10–11). You do not know which way to go. You choose one road, only to find that it leads into a cul-de-sac. You retrace your steps, try the other road, and, lo and behold, you find that the road leads in the direction you want. Two things have happened. First, you have learned how to handle the forked road problem and so will be able to deal with it in the future. Second, however, the new road will open up fresh choices, fresh problems. There is no end to the creation of problems and the finding of provisional solutions. But that is life.

It is worth illustrating this with a practical example. The light fails to work – one is stopped in the activity one was engaged in. How to solve the problem? One recalls a previous occasion. The light was not switched on at the plug. Therefore, one tries that switch. The light still does not work. Again, one recalls a situation. A new light bulb! The light still does not work. One recalls, again, a similar problem. The fuse is changed – and the light goes on. The problem, therefore, is met by a series of actions adopted as 'hypotheses' to be tested out in experience. Each action is informed by previous experiences, stored (in this case) consciously, which enable one to make connections. 'Knowledge' has been built up – that is, experience has been organized in such a way that it enables one to form appropriate actions, which are then tested out through further experience.

The adaptation is often helped by another person, who, seeing that the young apprentice cannot saw the wood or bend the pipe, shows how it can be done. The apprentice internalizes, or adapts to, this new way of behaving and therefore can deal successfully with similar situations in the future. Much of growing up is like this, adapting to problems as a result either of being shown how or of following examples. And in simpler social situations and societies, such adaptation requires no formal schooling.

In the light of such an analysis, Dewey seeks to avoid the dualism between the physical and the mental. The teleological explanation (the purposive nature of the response within a context of a changing and complex interpretive system, itself the product of previous responses to problems) is integral to what we mean by an organism. That is, the organism, the learning person, responds purposefully to new stimuli, but does so within an internalized system of interpretation. That interpretive system is the product of responses to previous problems, and transforms the very purposes, or 'ends-in-view', of the continued, though changed, activity. The world is *the experienced world* to which the organism is constantly having to adapt, thereby changing the reactive patterns to further stimuli. The organism lives in this world of 'meaning'. This can be referred to as an 'interpretive schema' through which we organize the world (part of which schema being notions of cause and effect) and solve the problems we are daily encountering. Knowing is a kind of doing and of dealing with problems. The world is what we interact with, and do things to, in the light of our system of interpretation. Such knowledge develops in accordance with the success or lack of success of the interaction with that world, which, when encountered, constantly blocks the path we have embarked upon – thus creating the problems that need to be overcome. Life is a series of problems to be overcome.

One must remember, also, that those interpretive schemata are of many kinds – what we would categorize as religious, poetic, artistic, scientific, and so on. Formal distinctions between different kinds of knowledge may have practical use (that itself needs to be tested out), but such practical use must not be elevated (as in traditional learning) to 'objective' or formal significance disconnected from their usefulness in helping the learner to overcome problems and to adapt more successfully to further experience. There is a holistic way of seeing the 'adaptive system of experience', pointing to a unity of poetry and science, reminiscent of that recounted in T.H. Green's *Prolegomena to Ethics* (1883), by which Dewey was much influenced, where poetry *feels* the unity and the relevance of a range of experiences clarified by science. Similarly, religion provides an aspiration to unity of thinking and explanation.

'Knowing how' and 'knowing that'

I have spoken of 'knowledge'. By this is meant the organization of experience in such a way that it enables the organism to deal with further experiences successfully in pursuing its course of action. It is a perception of those connections of an object which determine its applicability in a given situation ... An ideally perfect knowledge would represent such a network of interconnections that any past experience would offer a point of advantage from which to get at the problem presented in a new experience.

(DE, p. 340)

It would be easy for the reader to interpret such a passage as, once again, the knower, the spectator, being consciously aware of the interconnections and then acting accordingly. It would be back to the dualism of the mind (which has the 'perception' of connections) and the body (which provides the experiences that need to be connected). But the distinction between 'knowing how' and 'knowing that' has been articulated exhaustively in philosophy, especially since Gilbert Ryle's detailed analysis of it in his *Concept of Mind* (1949). 'Knowledge that' is reflected in propositions that have been verified by experience. 'Knowledge how' reflects the capacity to act appropriately in given situations. One talks of *knowing how* to ride a bicycle, to paint, to conduct a conversation with the Queen, to play football. Such knowledge may not be put into propositions. Indeed, the propositional knowledge about riding a bicycle (the laws of balance), about painting (the laws of perspective), about talking to the Queen (the rules of propriety) or about playing football (the dissection of strategy) may be written by people who are incapable of so behaving. Furthermore, those engaged in the activities of riding, painting, meeting the Queen and playing football may well be totally incapable of explaining what they are doing. Further, it may be the case that, in trying to do so, they make their performance worse. They fail to reach their 'ends-in-view'.

For example, the person who knows how to drive a (non-automatic) car is skillful at changing gear, knowing from the sound of the engine when to move into a higher or lower gear, letting in the clutch a split second before the gear change. There is a unity of action between sight, hearing, feeling with the feet and with the hand. Such unity of action could be described propositionally. It could be undertaken consciously, reviewing these propositions in one's mind. But one can be fairly certain that if one did, one would crash the gears. While learning to change gears as a total novice, the learner driver may very well be told to be conscious of what he or she was doing – to attend to the sound of the engine, etc. But through practice this 'knowledge' is internalized, goes beyond the description in its unity of enaction. It is translated into a habit, thereby freeing the motorist to attend to further purposes that are opened up and made possible by the newly formed 'know-how', embodied within a habit.

The distinction between 'knowing that' and 'knowing how' is an important one for making sense of Dewey, especially his criticisms of much educational practice. The primacy of one over the other, from the points of view of both epistemology and educational practice, has been a matter of controversy. Can 'knowing how' be logically reduced to 'knowing that' – that is, can the knowledge component implicit in the 'knowing how' be analyzed into a set of propositions or 'knowing that' (what Ryle referred to as the 'intellectualist legend')? Or is it the other way around: the 'knowing that' being ultimately analyzed into a lot of 'knowing hows'? Dewey would take the latter position. The propositional knowledge is inevitably an attempt to formulate the implicit experience that is embodied in our purposive activities. As such, it serves a very useful purpose. So long as its logical connection with experience is maintained, it can feed into that intelligent doing, albeit not capturing it in all its accumulated experience.

Educationally, of course, this is the basis of the criticism of those who in fact give primacy to 'knowing that' – to the curriculum, which is about transmitting the formulation of experience in propositions. That transmission, disconnected from the 'knowing how', from which it arises and which it seeks to formulate, has lost its vital function. It becomes a word game, no longer serving the active concerns from which it arose.

Inquiry

Inquiry is the process that takes place when the person faces a problem that is not easy to resolve. That problem can be of many kinds. Often it is a sense of puzzlement, and the person concerned struggles to make sense. The internal organization of experience is upset, as it were. New events or interventions by others do not fit in with the schema through which experience is understood or interpreted.

Education is concerned with providing the experiential capacity to make sense and to overcome the problem or puzzlement. Hence, as is argued in *Experience and Education* (p. 25), there is an 'organic connection between education and personal experience'. Education is part of that search for meaning – that trying to make sense.

Science and religion are equal partners in that search for the meaning of the experienced world. And in that search for meaning, one has to accept that our lives are more social than individual; through education we have a personal share in the social traditions of which we are part, drawing upon those traditions to make sense, to solve problems and to find meaning – a point that will be dealt with in Chapter 5, where the relationship is considered between the personal world of the learner *as experienced* and the public world of knowledge, which arises from the inquiries of other people who have gone before us. Hence, inquiry is that attempt 'to make sense', but to do so in the light of what other people have concluded in similar circumstances.

This process of inquiring, this reconciliation of the personal puzzlement and the public resources that help with a solution, is best described in Dewey's works *Logic: The Theory of Inquiry* (1938) and *How We Think* (1910, revised 1933). The first is essentially philosophical, giving a comprehensive account of his theory of knowledge and of logic, and the connection of these with the developments in science. The second had a wider audience in view and addressed more directly educational issues.

In *Logic: The Theory of Inquiry*, Dewey talks of inquiry in this way: 'Inquiry effects existential transformation and reconstruction of the material with which it deals; the result of the transformation . . . being conversion of an indeterminate problematic situation into a determinate resolved one' (LTI, p. 159). Or, again, for those who have not understood the above description of 'inquiry', 'Inquiry is the controlled or directed transformation of an indeterminate situation into one that is so determinate in its constituent distinctions and relations as to convert the element of the original situation into a unified whole' (LTI, p. 104). Such complex descriptions or definitions require a great deal of unpacking.

The main features of this 'existential transformation and reconstruction' are: (1) the obstacle to action, which is called a *problem*; (2) the marshaling of ideas or plans of action through which that

problem might be resolved, which is called an *inquiry*; (3) the 'existential' transformation of the problematic situation, which is symbolized
in the final judgment, or *warranted assertion*. At all three stages, action
enters into the very meaning of what it is to inquire (or to think, for
all thinking is an aspect of inquiring). A problem is a 'forked road
situation', where an organism's habit of action is inhibited by some
obstacle; hypothetical suggestions or ideas of alternative actions are
formulated which would remove the obstacle to action; the final judgment is the 'existential transformation' of the conditions such that
the activity may proceed. Hence, an 'indeterminate situation' – one
that creates a puzzle or a problem that needs to be resolved – is transformed into one where that puzzlement is removed and where the
'solution' re-establishes the essential unity of the situation. Relations
are re-established; things are seen as a whole. Life can continue, as it
were. Oppositions (or 'dualisms') have been overcome.

Thinking is 'intellectualized action'; it arises only when the habit
of action is broken – when one has got stuck. The relation of thought
to practical problems is logical, not contingent; the reference to
practical problems must enter into any characterization of thinking.
Hence, there is no real distinction between the theoretical and the
practical, the one being an offshoot of the other. And this is not just
an evolutionary account of the genesis of thought, or of the value
of practical thinking in preference to theoretical; it is an account of
what it *means* to think.

The process of inquiring is in one sense like the interaction of any
organism with its environment; plants and animals are programmed
to absorb the environment and adapt to it (and change it) – what
Scheffler refers to as the environment's 'organic energies'. But with
the human organism, that overcoming of contradictions and oppositions, that resolution of the puzzle or problem, is 'controlled or
directed'. As Scheffler states, 'Experience, for Dewey, is rather the
result of an *interaction* between objective conditions and organic energies, and is educative, as scientific experimentation is ideally, to the
extent that it engages the active deliberation, imagination, and motivation of the organism' (1973, p. 150). There is in Dewey, therefore,
a defining of experience that is not entirely based on the normal
usage of the word (see pages 23–4 on what is meant by 'defining'),

but involves a degree of stipulation within a broader philosophical understanding of 'thinking', 'knowledge creation' and 'inquiring'. There is a coherent system of ideas that requires a slight shifting of how we normally understand these terms. 'Experience' has the overtones of Dewey's understanding of scientific method; 'experience' contains elements of 'experimentation'. The child experiencing the new toy is experimenting with it: testing out what he or she can do with it and internalizing the consequences of the actions upon it, thereby leading to new 'experiments'. The child, as with the scientist, confronts a difficulty (the toy does not do what it should be doing); there is a problem, a testing out of a solution (the formulation of a hypothesis, albeit in a purely practical and unarticulated way), the manipulation of the toy and environment, the resolution of the problem – or possibly tears when the changed action still doesn't work. But if it does work, then the child is 'warranted' to proceed accordingly. The adult is 'warranted' to assert the provisional solution to the problem, which will then guide further activity.

The term 'warranted assertion' is important. The satisfaction of the inquiry lies not in a 'true proposition'; that would smell suspiciously like the dualistic conception of mind and body, of description and of described, of 'knowledge that' and of the object corresponding to that knowledge statement. Rather, it is the state of mind that enables one to go forward in the light of the experience that one has internalized. It is an 'existential transformation of experience', not a proposition.

In talking about the 'existential transformation of experience', resulting in 'warranted assertion' arising from 'inquiry', Dewey's analysis would seem to dodge questions about 'truth' and 'evidence', an accusation that was raised by Russell. In many respects, Dewey would, in reply, have claimed to be reconstructing the problem – a matter that should be subjected to considerable scrutiny and that will be considered at much greater length in Chapter 7.

Thinking and believing

The above argument and analysis are so important to an understanding of Dewey's philosophy of education that it is worth going over the same ground in a slightly different way, with particular reference to what he said in *How We Think*. The settled state of mind about how to act, and about what to expect as a consequence of acting, is called belief. One has many beliefs that are never articulated or rendered conscious through reflection. When I got up this morning I instinctively moved to the bathroom. I did not consciously think, 'The bathroom is at the end of the hall', but I believed it to be so because otherwise I would not have moved in that direction. Beliefs that govern our actions remain until the expected consequence fails to occur. I believe that my toothbrush will be in the bathroom, until experience no longer warrants that belief. 'Thinking' is the attempt to arrive at a state of belief.

Dewey, in the opening chapter of *How We Think*, distinguishes the various meanings that loosely we give to 'thinking' – including simply observing. But in making these distinctions he restricts the meaning that he wishes to attach to 'thinking' to that which goes beyond mere observation. Thinking aims at solving problems, at going beyond present experience in order to resolve a situation. It aims at belief, given that existing beliefs have been disturbed by some contradictory experience (which could, of course, have been the experience of what one has read or of what another person has related).

'Reflective thinking' is where one seeks to establish these beliefs systematically: 'Active, persistent, and careful consideration of any belief or supposed form of knowledge in the light of the grounds that support it, and the further conclusions to which it tends, constitutes reflective thought' (HWT, p. 6). Such thinking – that is, the systematic reflection on beliefs, their articulation and clarification, their consideration in the light of existing evidence, their understanding in the light of the perceived consequences of holding such beliefs, and the 'experimenting' to find out whether those consequences do in fact follow – does not come naturally or easily. It requires effort and training. It requires education. To be systematic, one has to control as far as possible the conditions under which observation is to take place as one tests out a possible way forward. It also requires the sort of community in which such systematic experimentation, in the light of evidence and criticism, is encouraged – a point that emphasizes the need for democratic communities, as I shall explain in Chapter 6.

All this might seem appropriate for adults. As Dewey points out in Chapter 3 of *How We Think*, adults already have a life (domestic, business, social) in which they are forever seeking 'ends-in-view' that constantly elude them, requiring therefore the overcoming of problems and the shifting of beliefs about the value of the ends they are pursuing and about the effectiveness of the means. That is not so obviously the case with children, for whom activities in which they will be trained to think reflectively and systematically need to be organized. Indeed, an exponent of Dewey's philosophy of education, W.H. Kilpatrick, developed what he referred to as 'the project method' to deal with this. There is a need therefore to select activities that have truly educative significance. Such activities would be those

> (a) which are most congenial, best adapted, to the immature state of development; (b) which have the most ulterior promise as preparation for the social responsibilities of adult life; and (c) which at the same time, have the maximum of influence in forming habits of acute observation and of consecutive influence.
>
> (HWT, p. 44)

Lacking here in this threefold account of an 'educative activity', though not excluded either, is the potential such activities have for drawing upon 'the accumulated wisdom of the race', as that is embodied in the formulated bodies of knowledge that we have inherited – a matter that Dewey makes much of elsewhere (see Chapter 5).

In so thinking, people attribute signs or indicators to otherwise natural objects. Clouds are signs of rain, although as a result of experience (for example, where cloudy skies are not followed by rain) the system of signs becomes increasingly more complex. Because of different background experiences, people will read into experiences different meanings; the same objects will signal different possible consequences. Through education, particular objects will acquire different meanings: the word 'crusade' conjures up different images, expectations and meanings among the followers of President Bush and the followers of Osama bin Laden. As Dewey explains, 'The child today soon regards as constituent parts of objects qualities that once it required the intelligence of a Copernicus or a Newton to apprehend' (HWT, p. 18).

Often such thinking does not take place, because existing states of belief are too precious to give up. Emotionally one cannot bear to have them shaken. One carries on believing despite contrary experience, or one reinterprets that experience in the light of existing beliefs. There is dependence on authority or on tradition. Or (in the absence of education) the cultural resources to challenge beliefs or to imagine and test out alternatives are lacking.

Religious and aesthetic experience

It may be thought that, in adopting 'the experimental method' as the way of pursuing inquiry and as the way of testing the meaning and 'warranted assertion' of ideas, Dewey, and those who subscribe to his pragmatic theory of meaning, would reject those kinds of inquiry and truth claims that are not so obviously to be tested against experience. This would seem quintessentially to apply to aesthetics (the justification and accounts of art), and religious claims and modes of inquiry. Why should he not follow, in this matter, the path of the logical positivists and deny the meaning (despite the truth-claiming nature of aesthetic and religious language) of such statements?

Dewey did not do so, and indeed that was partly because of the very pragmatic position he held. Art and statements about art, and religion and statements about religion (in theology, for example), had a practical use. They had a function in the personal and the social organization of experience.

Dewey had been brought up in a strictly religious household, but shortly after he commenced his university career his religious faith seems to have disappeared. He no longer believed in God transcending this world and acting as the source of goodness as well as being the arbiter of what counts as a good life and right action. There had to be a different source of morality. Indeed, belief in such a transcendent God created other kinds of dualism: that between the spiritual and the material worlds and that between the ideal of holiness (as, for example, in the 'Imitation of Christ') and the inadequate efforts of the sinner. Indeed, he was particularly incensed by the Protestant theologian Niebuhr's contrasting view, which emphasized the sinfulness of humankind, in contrast with the goodness and holiness of God (see Niebuhr, 1932). The chasm between the two destroyed the idea of hope and progress, and 'faith in the common man'.

More seriously from the philosophical point of view, however, Dewey viewed with suspicion institutional religion, because it substituted authority for 'experimentalism'. Experience, including 'religious experience', should always be provisional, open to further elaboration and meaningfulness following further experience and criticism, constantly overhauled.

And yet there remained a certain religious dimension to his life and work – if we use 'religious' in a broad and rather elastic sense. The search for a more inclusive meaning of experience, for the connection and interrelationship of experiences and above all for 'a common faith' (the title of a book he published in 1934) had something of a religious nature about it. Religion had a function. It had a practical part to play in our lives. It brought together and gave meaning to otherwise disparate experiences. Dewey's theory of meaning was not reduced to that of the logical positivists, whereby the meaning of a proposition lay in its mode of verification and where only empirical and logical modes of verification were admitted. He shared their views about the centrality of experience. However, the meaning of statements lay not in their somehow picturing or mirroring the world which itself existed independently of that picturing, but in their function or practical effect. *A Common Faith* showed an almost religious faith in the 'common man'.

Art, too, in its various forms, was of interest to Dewey in terms of its social and personal function rather than in terms of any distinctive 'aesthetic' qualities. Just as he was not really interested in the expositions of theologians (that is, in a distinctive form of knowledge concerned with religion), so too he was not interested in a separate form of knowledge concerned with the appreciation and evaluation of what are called works of art. Art objects had meaning because they played a part in our organization and anticipation of experience.

They were not something set apart, although galleries and museums made them often seem so. Indeed, that 'setting apart' of works of art helped to create a language about art, and attitudes to art, which were cut off from ordinary experience, and which created divisions, rather than closer relations, between people. To put it crudely, the self-styled aesthetes would distance themselves from those who were seen to lack their sensibility.

That role that art plays in everyday life was developed by Dewey in his book *Art as Experience*, also published in 1934. Indeed, he wanted to depict art as intimately related to, and continuous with, our experience of everyday life, not something pure in its disconnection from it. Thus, in *Art as Experience* he writes:

> The intelligent mechanic engaged in his job, interested in doing well and finding satisfaction in his handiwork, caring for his materials and tools with genuine affection, is artistically engaged. The difference between such a worker and the inept and careless bungler is as great in the shop as it is in the studio.
>
> (quoted in Ryan, 1995, p. 256)

Why is the mechanic artistically engaged? It is because he or she is not indifferent to the feel and to the appearance of the objects used and experienced. They have an effect on the mechanic. He or she experiences the same things differently from someone who does not have these feelings. And such feelings are tied to the colors and shapes and sounds that are the very stuff of ordinary experience. Hence, art or the recognition of art in ordinary experience provides certain sorts of connections. It organizes experience in a particular way, helping to anticipate further experiences, making experience meaningful in a different way.

But Dewey seems to want to go further than that, for experiencing in this way gives a sense of satisfaction, a fulfillment of desires, the conclusion of a search for meaning (even if provisional), a sense of wholeness that makes one want to linger over that which has this effect. And as one lingers, so one comes to see other features of the object (whether artificially created or natural), which enhances that experience. And in this, Dewey, I think, would want to blur that further dualism between the work of art (that which has been self consciously created) and the natural object, for the meaning of both lies in the effect that they have, that effect being one of drawing experiences together in some satisfying whole and of transforming how one then enjoys other experiences.

Hence, both religion and art reflect a certain way of experiencing, of seeing otherwise disparate experiences as a whole and in a particular way. They have an effect, and therefore, in that respect, have meaning. They have to be understood in terms of their function in everyday personal and social life. Recognizing them as meaningful in that sense does not require any commitment to a knowledge of religion (as claimed by theologians) or to a knowledge of art (as claimed by aestheticians). Therefore, they must have a place in education, but not the exalted place that is implicit in their being treated as distinct forms of knowledge. Young people will have the potential to experience in an aesthetic way the world of colors and shapes, whether natural or artificial. And that mode of experiencing needs to be both respected and fostered; it provides a satisfaction of certain tendencies and wants and it enables (as in the case of the mechanic) certain activities to be carried out in a particular way. The religious way of looking at things also has a function in shaping how we experience, and that way of experiencing needs to be acknowledged and opened to further development through further experience.

There is a sense in which that earlier religious mode of seeing things remained a powerful influence on how Dewey continued to experience the world, long after he had abandoned specific beliefs.

Conclusion

The concept of 'experience' as defined by Dewey is central to his philosophy in general and to his philosophy of education in particular. Persons are higher forms of organisms interacting with an environment that provides both the conditions for development and the obstacles to it. Such an organism, like all others, is actively seeking its survival. In so doing, it needs to adapt to the environment with which it interacts. Such interactions leave their mark. They in some way transform the organism, thereby affecting how it will continue to interact with the environment, both changing and being changed by it.

Persons incorporate such interactions in a much more sophisticated way through the development of habits and through organizing and anticipating the interactions in a more complex way, thereby becoming more able to control the environment or react to it fruitfully. An experience is a sort of mark upon the person, thereby both interpreted by the existing organization of previous experiences and transforming how the person sees the way forward in his or her continuing purposive activity. Furthermore, not only will the means to the end be reorganized, but also the 'ends-in-view' themselves.

What is distinctive of persons is their capacity to reflect upon these interactions, to articulate the organization of experience, and in particular to interact with the ways in which others have made sense of them. That is, there are social interactions as well as physical ones. Those reflections within a public arena enable persons to set them down propositionally – to create bodies of knowledge. But such bodies of knowledge are always provisional, always open to adaptation as they fail to resolve the new problems that arise. Their assertion and their transformation of the current way of experiencing are always provisional.

Furthermore, such warranted assertions arise from reflection on experience, and their meaning must therefore always be seen in relation to those experiences. They have no validity except in relation to them. The propositions of science, though often set down in textbooks and learned as such, are logically related to the actions on the environment that gave rise to them and to the very instruments through which the scientific inquiry was conducted.

Educationally, therefore, we need to get away from the transmission of other people's 'warranted assertions' as such and to see how these relate to the experiences that at a basic level we all share as human, living, surviving organisms. They must be related to the problems that gave rise to them. The alternative view would be to retreat to a philosophical position that espoused the dualism of mind and body, the position of either the classical empiricists or the rationalists. But that, for Dewey, contained so many insuperable problems – and problems that have been dissolved by recognition of the evolutionary conception of the human species.

Educationally, too, we need to identify those experiences which get in the way of further development and which arrest growth. As he says,

> Any experience is miseducational that has the effect of arresting or distorting the growth of further experience. An experience may be such as to engender callousness; it may produce lack of sensitivity and of responsiveness. Then the possibilities of having richer experiences in the future are restricted.
>
> (EE, p. 24)

Indeed, it was implicit in Dewey's criticism of 'traditional education' that so much was miseducative. It discouraged young people from learning. It bored them, even when, in the pursuit of personal advantage, they knuckled down and worked for their examinations. Dewey, in rejecting his religious past, would not have talked of mortal sin. But had he done so, he would have put 'boring the learner' at the top of his list, for that was the biggest turn-off for further learning and thus growth.

There are inevitably problems to be found in Dewey's solution to the problem he articulated, and these will be examined in Chapter 7. Are all puzzles and problems an arresting of an activity? What about, for example, the contemplative moments or the aesthetic ponderings? That does seem to be stretching the idea of an 'arrested action'. There are problems, too, over the conception of the replacement of 'truth' with 'warranted assertion' and of the distinction between theory and practice.

But its key message to education is the assertion of experience as a crucial element in the development of understanding and of the meaning attached to experience. Experience is not a passive reception of a sense datum, but an interpretation of what happens based on previous experiences and transforming how one interprets further experiences.

The significance of the young person's experience is seen to be almost irrelevant as far as certain critics are concerned. If one is a 'traditionalist', as described in the previous chapter, then experience might be invoked, where that can be harnessed to the subject matter being taught as a way of motivating the learner, but there is no intrinsic connection between that which is thought worth teaching and the experiences that are brought to the classroom – or, preferably, left outside it. Indeed, so impoverished would many teachers feel those experiences to be that they would see them as obstructions to an education which should instead initiate the young person into forms of understanding that are worthwhile in themselves, however disconnected from the experience of the learner.

This is not so hard to imagine. Indeed, it characterizes much that passes for education. How little of the experiences of the young people in an inner-city school (the experience of asylum seeking, of being victim to racism or harassment of one kind or another) is built on in the classroom where 'personal, social and health education' or 'social studies' is taught.

O'Hear disdainfully dismisses Dewey's emphasis on the importance of experience:

> In Dewey we also find sentimental talk of the value of the experience of the child, of the intrinsic significance of every growing experience. Classrooms become miniature Swiss cantons in which everything is up for discussion and negotiation by the whole population. The teacher is no more than a provider of 'suggestions', a 'facilitator' in today's jargon.
>
> (1991, p. 26)

Whatever the criticisms one might direct against Dewey (and such criticisms would need to focus upon the underlying philosophical position – something delayed to Chapter 7), O'Hear's criticism would not be one. Education was conceived as that search for meaning – that trying to make sense. To ignore the experience of the young person – how he or she saw and understood the world, made connections and anticipated the future – would be to fail to educate. One might succeed in sticking on bits of 'knowledge', as it were, but the person, as he or she interacted with the physical and social world, would be left untouched. No connections would have been made.

Chapter 4

Child-centered Education

Dewey's critics

The suspicion, if not antagonism, that the mention of Dewey raises in people's minds, reflected in the statement of Keith Joseph (see page 3) or in the writing of Professor O'Hear (see page 4), is nothing new. It dogged Dewey in his own lifetime. Indeed, many of his lectures and writings (in particular, *Experience and Education*, published in 1938) were a constant defense of the 'New Education' (as he constantly called it) against critics who saw his educational philosophy as dangerous and subversive.

Why was such a mild-mannered and scholarly man seen as being so dangerous? It is interesting to note that a similarly modest and scholarly follower of Dewey's ideas, Dr Pat Wilson of Goldsmiths College, London, was also accused of being dangerous and subversive when exposing Dewey's ideas to in-service courses for teachers in the 1970s. His book *Interest and Discipline in Education* (Wilson, 1971) remains one of the best expositions of Dewey's thinking, but at a dramatic session of the Philosophy of Education Society of Great Britain in 1970 his paper was dismissed with less than philosophical decorum by the custodians of a more traditional view of educational aims (Wilson, 1974). Education in the then currently orthodox view was about the initiation of young people into the different forms of knowledge, and that certainly could not happen if young people were allowed, under the guise of education, to pursue their own interests. Professor O'Hear's paper given to the Applied Philosophy Society in 1988 similarly dismissed Dewey as subverting the central aim of education as an initiation into the cultural richness we have inherited (O'Hear, 1988).

What lay at the center of this antagonism was and is Dewey's so-called child-centered approach to teaching. This did seem to subvert traditional understandings of what education is about, and also the practices that such beliefs led to. It was, for example, argued that under the influence of child-centered education, many young people were denied the opportunity to gain the knowledge and skills that would enable them to have a good understanding of the world in which they lived and in which they had to earn a living. By being allowed to pursue those activities that interested them, they failed to learn those things that really mattered. And, indeed, there were some dramatic examples of educational failure as a result of so-called child-centered practices, illustrated in Britain through the case of the William Tyndale school, which was the subject of the very thorough Auld Report (1976).

Being child-centered was understood by the opponents of Dewey's ideas and practice as equivalent to letting the children take up the command position in education: to decide on the interests to be pursued, to shape the curriculum to be followed in the development of those interests, and to decide when those interests had reached their end, as far as the child was concerned, and then to be supplanted by other, often ephemeral interests. The value of those interests lay simply in the fact that they were interesting, even if only temporarily. Indeed, behind such a view, not missed by the critics, there seemed a theory of value, according to which there were no objective criteria, external to the wants and wishes of the child, that justified the superior value of those subjects, traditionally taught, if they were not of interest to the learner. The teacher meanwhile would be but a 'facilitator' of the child's learning in the pursuit of those interests. The child's interests were to be the focus and the shaper of the curriculum, and thus of the learning experience.

I wish to postpone the ethical criticisms to a later chapter. They are extremely important and require a complex answer if the accusation of moral relativism is to be avoided. Here I wish simply to argue that the rather simplistic account of child-centeredness, although prevalent in not a few educational writers and practitioners, was and is a total distortion of Dewey's thinking. Certainly he claimed to be 'child-centered'. Certainly, too, that child-centeredness required one to take seriously the interests of the child and to incorporate those interests into the learning program. Indeed, he argued as follows:

> Now the change which is coming into our education is the shifting of the centre of gravity ... In this case the child becomes the sun about which the appliances of education revolve; he is the centre about which they are organized.
>
> (SS, p. 103)

But further, as Dewey explained in 'My pedagogic creed', it was much more than the child becoming the center 'about which the appliances of education revolve'. Most teachers and educational planners would claim that. Rather, it was the distinctive interpretation of how the child should become 'the center' or 'the sun' around which everything revolved. That interpretation put the very impulses and inclinations of the child as the determinants of the learning to take place: 'The child's own instincts and powers furnish the material and give the starting point for all education' (MPC, p. 45). The difficulties here lie in Dewey being placed within what is referred to as a child-centered tradition of education shared by such figures as Rousseau, Froebel, Pestalozzi, Montessori and, in recent times, A.S. Neill. They have, indeed, many features in common, which is what causes them to be lumped together, but there are also significant differences – one being, as I shall elaborate upon in Chapter 6, the importance that Dewey attached to the social and community context of individual growth. Another significant difference is the distinctive philosophical and pragmatist base to Dewey's position, which I shall analyze in Chapter 7.

What these different educationalists have in common is the importance of the activity and interests of the child as the starting point of education – indeed, as the very 'things' that need to be educated. Such activities and interests should not be seen, as they so often are, as getting in the way of education. Nor should they be seen as things to be harnessed, for motivational purposes, to what the teacher wants the child to learn but which the learner is not interested in. Rather, the activities and interests that are natural to the child are the focus of educational progress. As John Darling explained in his book on child-centered education, what the different exponents of child-centered education had in common was 'to think of education in terms of "natural" development: the nature of the child, it seems, is geared towards learning. Another side of this claim about children is that they are natural doers, makers and creators' (1994, p. 3). For Dewey, this was epitomized in the importance to be attached to the identification and development of the interests that children naturally acquire and through the pursuit of which learning takes place. However, his understanding of 'having an interest' and of developing such an interest distinguishes him from other child-centered educationalists with whom he is too often confused. The best way to understand what he meant is to see how he responded to the four kinds of problem raised by his critics.

The first problem lay in the failure of his critics to understand what an 'interest' is or could be. It is not to be confused with 'whim' or temporary fancy. To be interested in something means more than paying a 'passing attention' to it. It is something that incorporates an understanding, a valuing and a potential for further and deeper involvement. Furthermore, it is something that can be disciplined, and must be disciplined if that interest is to be maintained and brought to the fulfillment that it first promised.

The second problem lay in the failure of the critics to link the pursuit of an interest with an understanding of the child – with the 'impulses' that are intrinsic to a child's nature and that are central to the development of his or her very being.

The third problem lay in the failure of his critics to appreciate the essentially social nature of the growth of the child – of the disciplining of those very impulses that direct activities. Child-centered education is often interpreted as a focus on the individual as an autonomous person, actually or potentially so. But that is to ignore the essentially social nature of each individual and the crucial part that the social context of each individual plays in the development or frustration of his or her growth – to the creation and maintenance of the different interests.

The fourth problem that is raised by critics concerns the limited nature of many young persons' interests. There are other possible interests which the learners do not in fact have, which have much greater potential for worthwhile learning and which it is the responsibility of the teacher to create and nurture. To put it simply: the learner may have no interest in history, but the teacher believes that historical understanding is worthwhile and thus tries to create an interest.

I shall pursue each of these problems in turn.

The concept of 'interests'

To be interested in something, as I have said, means more than taking a passing fancy to it. To say that someone is interested in something is to say that that person attends to its features, seeks to know a little more, is motivated to pursue the interest further. Without the right kind of help at the right moment, that interest might evaporate; it is too difficult to continue with, frustration sets in, alternative interests seem less demanding, or there is not the motivating and wider social encouragement to continue. Part of the interest lies in the cognitive demands that the object of interest makes upon the interested party – one wants to know what it will lead on to or what the solution is to a problem felt.

Such attention to the further possibilities of an interest make it difficult for the outsider to identify exactly what the person is interested in – what the precise identity is of that which holds the attention. Wilson (1971, 1974) explores this in some detail. It may seem obvious, for example, that Henry is interested in football (soccer); he plays a lot with his friends. But what aspects of playing football interest him? It could be that playing football is but a means to impress his friends or to find companionship in a common pursuit. On the other hand, the real interest could be the opportunity offered to play a competitive team sport where football (soccer) is the only one available. The interest might lie in the possibility of earning a living through turning professional. Or it could lie in the intrinsic skill of the game: the passing, the dribbling, and the scoring of goals. A proper description of an interest would need to give this fuller account, and in each case the description would be sufficiently different as to indicate different interests. And in each case the identification of the exact interest could not come from a straightforward observation of what the person is doing.

It takes an experienced teacher, therefore, and one who knows the child well, to identify what the interest really is – indeed, to help the young person to recognize the nature of the interest, which is only dimly perceived. The experienced teacher is able to help the learner to understand that interest, to develop it, not to be frustrated in its pursuit, to build upon it and to see its possibilities. And such possibilities might be legion. In following an interest, the learner needs to overcome problems, to obtain further understanding, to acquire more skills, to acquire discipline and perseverance. For example, for an initial interest in cooking (an example frequently given by Dewey; see SS, p. 106) to be maintained requires the acquisition of basic principles (the different ways of using heat for different purposes or the thickening of liquids). Boredom, the antithesis of having an interest, will set in if that initial knowledge does not become more sophisticated and if new recipes are not tried out. There seems no limit to how that interest might develop, as the beginner cook becomes more precise and scientific in the preparation of food, or comes to see the wider social significance of preparing meals.

The good teacher knows when to intervene, providing that extra knowledge and help where the learner gets stuck. He or she knows, too, the possibilities of certain interests that are likely to lead down culs-de-sac, and of those interests that will lead to 'an open road'. Such a teacher knows also when not to intervene, lest to do so might kill the interest. Hence, the pursuit of interests, as a hallmark of child-centered education and as understood by Dewey, was a far cry from how his critics saw such a pursuit and from how it has come to be identified with child-centered schooling.

Interests and children's growth

These interests are founded upon the basic impulses which very young people have and which are at the basis of their growth as human beings. These impulses (sometimes referred to as 'interests') were outlined in Dewey's second essay in *The School and Society*, entitled 'The school and the life of the child' (pp. 109ff.). Dewey classified them under four headings: the impulses (or instincts, or tendencies) to:

- social intercourse, engagement in conversation, relating and responding to others
- finding out or inquiry, as problems are encountered or interests aroused
- making and creating – as reflected in play, in make-believe; in a range of activities, including construction of objects
- expression of thoughts and feelings in a concrete way through art and words.

All these impulses or tendencies or basic interests interlink. The desire to communicate might arise from the wish to find out; the impulse to make something might arise partly from the wish to express a feeling or an understanding. Indeed, the drawing or painting arises from several impulses within a young person engaged actively with the world and people around him or her.

Such impulses give rise to interests, to the pursuit of activities that engage the mind and that demand further activity, further conversation, further inquiry, further making and expression of thoughts and feelings. The good teacher sees the possibilities in such interests for further growth such that the learner will not become bored or frustrated. In seeing those possibilities, the teacher would perhaps help increase the relevant language skills so that better communication with others can take place, or provide technical help to progress the inquiry, or open up further possible ways in which the inquiry might go, or fire the imagination within the general area of interest.

The point is that each learner is essentially active through interests which direct that activity, which can be pursued only through increasing knowledge and skills, and which (properly directed) open up immense possibilities for future learning. Such impulses are not, in the main, idiosyncratic or esoteric. They are intrinsic to what it means to be and to develop as a human being: the impulse to engage with other people in various kinds of social relationship, the impulse to understand and make sense of the world and the relationships in which one lives, the impulse to create something in that world in which one gains a sense of achievement, the impulse through sound or behavior or art to express one's understanding and feelings.

There are, however, limits to how far those interests can be developed unaided within the family or household. Schools create the larger community, the place where social relationships can be expanded, where inquiry can be more effectively pursued, and where creating and constructing can be carried beyond a simple level. But essentially a school should be seen as that: as an extension and an enriching of the learning that has already taken place. As such, therefore, the school is a place for 'living primarily, and learning through and in relation to this living' (SS, p. 105).

So basic to the very being of the learner are such impulses and their development through various kinds of activity that to ignore them at school and to treat them as worthless is to show profound disrespect to the learner. It is to cut off the so-called educational process from the very core of the learner's being.

Dewey, therefore, is strongly critical of the typical school for being unable or unwilling to build on these interests. As he argues, 'The things that have to do with these processes have not even a recognized place in education. They are what the educational authorities who write editorials in the daily papers generally term "fads" and "frills"'. Indeed,

> There is very little space in the traditional schoolroom for the child to work. The workshop, the laboratory, the materials, the tools with which the child may construct, create and actively inquire, and even the requisite space, have been for the most part lacking.
>
> (SS, p. 101)

Such schools are marked by the stark and regimented way in which they are designed – made for listening, not for 'doing'; for passivity, not for active engagement; for dependency on whatever the teacher wants the student to learn, not for self-empowerment through inquiry and making.

Learners are treated with disrespect because their interests – what absorbs their growing minds, their curiosity, their drive to understand and to create – are treated as of no importance and to be ignored. However, it is equally disrespectful simply to harness those interests to what the teacher, not the learners, is interested in – to use those interests in order to motivate the learners to learn what is of no interest to them. The failure of 'traditional learning', in Dewey's eyes, is that, at its worst, it treats the young learner's thinking (what is of interest to the learner, what engages his or her concerns and aspirations) as of no educational interest; at its best, it acknowledges these, but solely as a way of manipulating the learner to learn what is of no interest. Interests should be not what are used; they are what should be educated. Otherwise, what the learner acquires at school is but the formulas, the words, the stories that he or she is required to take on board in order to satisfy the teacher or the school or the examination system, while they as persons remain basically unaffected by the so-called learning experience.

The social nature of interests

Very often the critics of child-centered education point to the misleading metaphors used, in particular the comparing of the young and growing child to a seed (an acorn, in the words of Froebel, 1886) that should be allowed to grow according to its nature. Perhaps, as with any seed, some assistance is required – some watering, some fertilizer, some propping up against the damaging winds. But basically the dominant metaphor arises from biology – more precisely, gardening.

Central, however, to Dewey's idea of human growth was the social context in which that growth necessarily took place. The biological metaphor of the seed or plant would be unacceptable. Growth, through the unfolding of impulses and the interests they gave rise to, was essentially social. In following the impulse to communicate, the child acquired the language of the family and society to which he or she belonged. That language, and thus the communication which took place, contained particular understandings and evaluations; it helped form the interests that were to develop. And in developing those interests, the young learner would be constantly interacting with others in the social group.

Similarly with the other impulses. To inquire into a problem or to find the solution to a puzzle, the learner is struggling to make sense on the backs of others who have been there before, who have shown the way and who have developed the conceptual and manual tools for further exploration, questioning and discovery. The development of the child through the pursuit of interests can take place up to a point within the home, especially where the home and the immediate environment are rich in the activities with which the young child is associated (for example, in the production and preparation of food or in the maintenance of the home or in the caring for livestock). But for many young people those opportunities are not easily available, or the home provides the appropriate environment only to a certain level. Therefore, the school should provide the environment where these interests can reach greater depths. The school ideally is the extension of the home and of the family, where the interest in communicating, in inquiring, in creating and making, and in expressing oneself can be extended and enhanced.

Directed interests

In the first of the three papers in *The School and Society*, Dewey speaks of the impoverishment of social experience as a result of the transition, which he had witnessed in his lifetime, from the culturally rich (even if economically poor) household industries to the larger, factory-based industries. Prior to the industrialization of work, children would grow up in an environment in which they would be in touch with the basic conditions of living – with the growth and production of the food they ate, with the sources and the weaving of the cloth they wore, with the creation and manufacture of the houses they lived in. From an early age they would be engaged cooperatively in these activities. The interest in them would be basic, because they were to do with survival and the gaining of some comfort. The interests would develop as they learned from their parents and their community how to meet these needs more skillfully, leading on to further possibilities. The social intercourse that would surround these activities would enable them to see the point of them and their cultural significance. They would be apprenticed not just to someone from whom they would learn certain skills, but to a form of life in which they would learn reciprocal duties and responsibilities.

The transition to a very different sort of society, which had gone on apace over a couple of generations, had cut young people off from that immediate and experiential acquaintance with the source of human survival in nature and with the struggle whereby people had learned to survive. This was particularly reflected in the lack of manual skills and activities in their lives and in their education. Certain human impulses were not fully realized; they were killed as soon as the children entered formal education. 'Thinking with the hands', which had always been the experience of most people, was now diminished if not altogether terminated in the formal education that had replaced the informal education of the family and community. In its place had been put talking about these things, disconnected from experience – symbols of reality rather than reality itself.

It is a mark of all within the 'child-centered tradition' to make once again this vibrant connection between experience and understanding – that is, between an active engagement with the natural world we inhabit and the knowledge of that world. Such an active engagement enables the learner to see the problems, to explore the solutions, to develop the requisite skills, to work with others in the common enterprise. The understanding that comes with this active involvement cannot be attained through standing apart or from reading about the processes in books.

It is interesting to reflect here how those who have achieved so much in engineering and science were themselves involved in making and doing, in working with their hands as well as 'with their brains'. William Morris (later Lord Nuffield) became the brilliant engineer who made the first Morris cars in Britain, as well as making a fortune in the 1930s when everyone else was losing money. He had left school at 15, is claimed thereafter never to have read a book, and would employ no one who had the theoretical knowledge gained from a university degree. That knowledge came, and had to come, from the practical doing and making, and from insight into principles through the practical engagement with the problem and through the critical appraisal of more experienced people.

Attempts, Dewey acknowledged, had been made to preserve practical activities for some on the curriculum (often the 'less academic') where they were thought to be useful: sewing for girls and woodwork for boys, who would need such skills for subsequent employment. But to cite such attempts would be to miss the point. The importance of these practical skills, which related to human interests and concerns,

lay in the deeper understanding of the human condition which they
opened up. Working in a kitchen and learning to cook would be
seen not as a useful activity (though indeed it would be a useful activity) but as a social and transforming experience through which team
spirit was developed, achievement demanded discipline, problems
had to be solved, the significance of food culturally and nutritionally
would be understood. Indeed, far from such active learning being
merely useful, its value is to be seen as a 'liberation from narrow
utilities ... openness to the possibilities of the human spirit that
makes these practical activities in the school allies of art and centers of science and history' (SS, p. 90).

A modern example of this would be the lessons to be seen at a
typical Steiner school. At Steiner schools the impulse to express is
highly respected. Art plays a significant part in the learning experience. But every aspect of the process needs to be experienced. In
creating clothes, the material has to be prepared. That preparation
may require the cleaning and carding of wool, and then the dye-
ing of the fabric. But where do the dyes come from? The students
create the dyes from the berries, which are in the trees and fields.
The interests generated in the pursuit of the activity give insight into
the nature of the materials, the human effort that historically was
required for survival, and the cultural artifacts through which per-
sonality was expressed and community values satisfied. Manual skills
were developed; problems were overcome; design criteria were met;
cooperation within teams was established. While this author observed
these processes happening, the 8-year-olds were outside preparing the
ground for sowing the seeds. Throughout the year they would tend
the gardens, watching and supporting the growth of the plants they
had sown and finally harvesting the fruit of their labor. Pure Dewey!
– for these children were happily and practically engaged together
in a purposeful project that demanded team effort, constant communication, the acquisition of manual skills and practical know-how,
familiarity with the very conditions of survival, and the beginnings of
'theory' in the sense of a knowledge of nature, its possibilities and its
dangers. Interests were developed with a knowledge base that would
very likely (but maybe not in everyone) grow into further satisfying
interest, both horticultural and cultural.

Hence, it is important to recognize that Dewey, despite the criticism of his child-centered theories, strongly advocated the direction of the interests which young people had, so that they would be rich sources of learning. Not any development of an interest would be the most beneficial educationally. The pursuit of an interest should lead, if it is properly directed, to a wider social outlook, to greater insight into the human condition, to an awareness of the social and economic conditions in which one had to live and find employment.

Several examples are given in his lectures *The School and Society* of how a simple interest can, under proper direction, give rise to the sort of inquiries that extend the knowledge located in the physical and social sciences. The rationale is as follows:

> [T]he little child who thinks he would like to cook has little idea of what it means or costs, or what it requires. It is simply a desire to 'mess around', perhaps to imitate the activities of older people ... But here, too, if the impulse is exercised, utilized, it runs up against the actual world of hard conditions to which it must accommodate itself; and there again come in the factors of discipline and knowledge.
>
> (SS, p. 106)

Dewey then goes on to give examples, one being that of cooking an egg, and how an understanding opened up a world of science and of nutrition – the experimenting with temperatures, the effect that these temperatures had upon the white of the egg. As Dewey explained, education lay in seeing the universal in the particular, thereby enhancing the likelihood of the interest reaching a greater depth and a more motivating desire to further learning:

> For the child to realize his or her own impulse by recognizing the facts, materials and conditions involved, and then to regulate his impulse through that recognition, is educative. This is the difference, upon which I want to insist, between exciting or indulging an interest and realizing it through its direction.
>
> (SS, p. 108)

This, of course, leads to some difficulties in the understanding of Dewey. He argues for education as the development of interests, those interests, at their most basic level, arising from the distinctive human impulses to communicate, to inquire, to express and to make. However, not any direction of such interests will suffice. There are certain directions that the teacher should ensure, namely those that give insight into the physical, social and moral worlds that the young learner inhabits. And those directions may not flow naturally out of the original impulses. It is that fact which the critics latch on to, and it is that criticism which Dewey so clearly deals with. But in doing so he does not seem, as would be the case with other child-centered theorists, to define the aims of education simply in relation to enabling the learners to satisfy their interests. Rather, there would seem to be a more complex ethical justification for the kinds of interests that Dewey thinks are worth pursuing.

Conclusion

Dewey was criticizing a 'system of education' that he saw to be distinctly *mis*educational. In treating young people as passive recipients of knowledge transmitted to them, that system failed to advance their understanding of, and involvement with, the physical and social world in which they had, for better or worse, to conduct their lives. They already were learners simply through living within communities, small though these may have been. They learned through the interests associated with living intelligently: solving problems, relating to others, making things and finding ways of expressing their feelings and thoughts. However, the traditional education to which they transferred at a certain age disconnected learning from life. It succeeded no doubt in distilling knowledge ready for transmission, but it failed to attend to the nature of the learner. It failed to see that the learners were already actively learning through their engagement with others and through the tasks they were undertaking. Furthermore, it failed to see that those very interests had the potential for further learning, and for enabling the young people to obtain greater insight into the world they were to live and work within.

To say that, and to translate it into a program of teaching and learning, required careful attention both to what, deep down, were those interests and to how they might be enriched, extended and directed. Interests arose from basic impulses and tendencies. They demanded attentiveness, activity, new knowledge and skills. They related to wider social activities. To place the child at the center, to regard him or her as the 'sun about which the appliances of education revolve', did not mean that the child should be allowed, undisciplined, to follow any fad or fancy. Nor did it mean that he or she would simply grow like the tender plant of Froebel so long as there was a little watering or weeding. Rather, those interests needed to be nurtured through being part of the social world to which the learner belonged. Connections had to be made with similar achievements and aspirations of others, present and past. Such achievements were part of the culture we have inherited, and so the job of the teacher was to make the connections between the active learning of the young people and the cultural inheritance that the teacher represented – the major theme of Chapter 5.

Chapter 5

Curriculum: Logical and Psychological Aspects

The problem: the child or the curriculum?

The regular criticism of Dewey, as with other educationalists who are referred to as 'child-centered', is that in pursuing their own interests, young people will not get the information, the knowledge, the theory, the understandings and the skills that are intrinsic to the different subjects and that are required for an informed and intelligent grasp of the physical and social worlds. That is why the 'traditional school' is so keen to transmit the knowledge that is deemed to be worthwhile. That is why the curriculum is divided up into packaged knowledge called subjects. There is so much knowledge to cover that it has to be transmitted in an organized and systematic way. Dewey, therefore, puts these words into the mouths of his critics: 'How, upon this basis, shall the child get the needed information; how shall he undergo the required discipline?' (SS, p. 117).

The answer to this I have already hinted at in Chapter 4. The serious interests of the child, arising from the impulses to make sense of the world, to understand what is necessary to live well, to engage with other people, to create and make things as part of the job of living, have, internal to them, their own discipline. They open up further demands for inquiry and for the skills required in making and creating. But they will introduce the young person, *if properly directed*, to the basic understandings and discipline formalized within the subjects. The difference is that whereas in traditional schooling that 'knowledge' will be essentially the manipulation of words and symbols on the basis of a learned formula, in the case of directed interests the knowledge will be integral to the learner's own inquiries and to an understanding of the activities he or she is engaged in. It will be part of living.

The difficulties in this, however, would seem to be many. First, the gulf is exceptionally wide between the interests of the young child and the knowledge that is embodied in the different subjects that normally make up the curriculum; indeed, there seems little logical or motivational connection. Second, even if, or where, such a connection can be made, the route from the initial interest to the knowledge and theoretical perspective within the different subjects would be practically impossible, unless very directed. Furthermore, is that not what the 'traditional education' did? In the transmitting of scientific knowledge (for example, the biological understanding of photosynthesis), the learner would come to see its connection with everyday living (for example, the growth and health of plants).

1.

2.

Few young people do see this connection, as Dewey pointed out. There is a gulf between the consuming interests of the young person and the knowledge that is transmitted in school. That knowledge is expressed in symbols, formulas and propositions totally disconnected from the experience of the young person. It is learned as such for purposes of passing examinations or pleasing the teacher, but leaves the learner untouched in his or her active living. It does not enter into intelligent grasp of the social and physical worlds in which the young person plays an active part.

The answer, within the child-centered tradition, has so often been to reject entirely the teaching of subjects – the transmission of bodies of knowledge – and to concentrate solely on the active interests of the child, whose growing understanding is not organized into neatly packaged subject boundaries. This is caricatured by Dewey in this way: 'The child is the starting-point, the center and the end. His development, his growth, is the ideal. *It alone furnishes the standard* ... Not knowledge, not information, but self-realization, is the goal' (CC, p. 127; my italics).

There are more recent versions of this view, as people try to make the curriculum 'more relevant' to the reluctant learner, and teach through interests, not through subjects, which are regarded rather disparagingly as mere 'social constructions' of those in a position of power to control how people should think.

Therefore, as Dewey argues in *The Child and the Curriculum*, a sharp contrast is drawn between two very different views of education – and a seemingly unbridgeable gulf between two different kinds of educational practice. On the one hand there are the ardent supporters of the transmission of the knowledge and culture we have inherited. Such knowledge and culture has been organized into logically discrete subjects with their own distinctive concepts, principles, essential facts, modes of inquiry. The teacher is both the custodian of such organized knowledge and the initiator of the next generation into it. Such initiation requires an organized and systematic transmission of knowledge on the part of the teacher, and on the part of the learner a struggle to make sense, an entry into a new and strange way of seeing the world. But once the learner is on the inside, as it were, he or she can be part of the expert world of scientists, sociologists, historians, mathematicians and others. On the other hand, there are those who see how disconnected such teaching remains from the actual thinking, aspirations and active interests of the recipients. Those should be the focus of the 'curriculum' – the period set aside to help the learner. 'The only significant method is the method of the mind as it reaches out and assimilates' (CC, p. 127). The teacher is but the facilitator of that process.

This, however, is one of the 'false dualisms' that Dewey so ardently argues against. He is as scathing of the child-centered conception of education, encapsulated in the mere pursuit of interests with the teacher as facilitator, as he is of 'traditional education', reflected in the transmission of 'packaged knowledge'. At the same time, he recognizes that each has an element of validity, and he believes that the curriculum should be a reconciliation of the two positions, for there are two fundamental factors in the educative process: 'an immature, undeveloped being; and certain social aims, meanings, values incarnate in the matured experience of the adult. The educative process is the due interaction of these forces' (CC, p. 123). This is not done by concentration on the one or the other or by giving one a place subordinate to the other or by setting one against the other (the child versus the curriculum). Rather, it is a matter of giving due regard to both the psychological aspects of learning and the logical structure of the subject matter. But, further, it is a matter of showing how the interest being actively and purposefully pursued by the young learner 'already contains within itself elements – facts and truths – of just the same sort as those entering into the formulated study' (CC, p. 129).

The psychological aspects of learning

A central feature of the child-centered tradition in its different forms is that education must begin with a careful study of the way in which the mind of the child develops: how the child comes to find his or her way around, to make sense of the surrounding world, to learn to assimilate new experiences and at the same time to adapt to them. There was seen to be a science of child development. The process of development thus identified – the natural life and growth of the child – should shape the educational process. That 'science of child development' provided help to this process, got rid of things that obstructed the process and facilitated progress to the next stage.

The science of child development, which also identified the goal of development as something intrinsic to the process itself, not externally imposed, is made explicit by Pestalozzi and Froebel, and became a hallmark of the New Education Fellowship, well described by Darling (1994), prior to the Second World War, whose international conferences attracted thousands of people from all over the world. That fellowship, as Darling argues, deeply influenced the Hadow Report (*The Primary School*, 1932) and indirectly influenced the Plowden Report (*Children and Their Primary Schools*, 1967), and particularly the colleges that trained future generations of teachers. The mood was clearly expressed by A.E. Campbell's *Report of the New Education Fellowship Conference*, held in New Zealand in 1937, quoted by Darling (1994, p. 36):

> The 'principle of activity' expresses the *empirically discovered truth* [my italics] that the child grows by his own efforts and his own real experience, whether it be in skill or knowledge, in social feeling or spiritual awareness. It is not what we do to the child that educates him, but what we enable him to do for himself, and this is equally true of the young infant, the school child and the adolescent.

The Hadow Report seemed to endorse the 'psychologizing' of the curriculum, arising from study of children's learning:

> In framing the curriculum for the primary school ... our main care must be to supply children between the ages of seven and eleven with what is essential to their healthy growth – physical, intellectual and moral – during that particular stage of their development. The principle which is here implied will be challenged by no one who has grasped the idea that life is a process of growth in which there are successive stages, each with its own specific character and needs.
> (Hadow Report, 1932, quoted in Darling, 1994, p. 39)

Education, therefore, begins with, and proceeds from, a study of child development which has its own laws and which embodies the very aims of the educational process. Psychology is therefore the key study in educational theory and the education of teachers. There remain strong elements of this view in the theory of Piaget's stages of intellectual development (see Piaget, 1926) and, indeed, of Kohlberg's stages of moral development (see Kohlberg, 1971).

This would seem to be also what Dewey initially believed in, with his emphasis (as described in the previous chapter) upon the development and growth of the child's interests as the aim of education: growth through the realization of the child's potential in the impulses to socialize, to inquire, to create and to express. But although it was central to Dewey's educational ideas that study of how young people develop and learn is crucial (what *interests* them, and thus what can be built upon those interests), it was also central that those interests needed to be directed and that the direction could not be found simply through a study of the interests themselves. That direction is to be found in the 'accumulated wisdom of the race'. That accumulated wisdom is formalized (stacked for ready access, if you like) in books and artifacts, unlike the knowledge that informs the understandings of the young learner. That accumulated wisdom is organized along very different principles from that which shapes the psyche of the learner. The latter is related to present or recent experience; it is shaped by practical and social concerns; it is integrated around personal interests, and colored by feelings and emotions. The former transcends immediate and personal experience; it is fragmented into logically distinct subject matters; and it is bereft of personal interest or emotion. But although the distinction can and must be made, Dewey argued that there were connections – logical connections – and that the educational process lay in establishing these and in recognizing that the psychological account of how young people think and the logical structuring of the wisdom of the race are but a continuum that needs to be understood and respected as such.

To understand that, we need to examine what is meant by the logical structure of the subject matter.

The logical aspects of learning

To learn is to learn something – a seemingly obvious point, but one frequently forgotten in the rhetoric of education. The claim is frequently made that the purpose of education is to help young people to learn how to learn. But the retort must surely be: 'to learn how to learn what?' To learn how to ride a bicycle is very different from learning how to be good, which is different again from learning to love romantic poetry, which is different again from learning algebra, which is different again from learning to understand the key aspects of the Enlightenment. To give an account of learning to ride a bicycle requires reference not only to the psychological process of learning but to the standards of performance that constitute riding a bicycle properly. To give an account of learning algebra requires statements not only about the 'struggle to understand', but also what counts as having understood: the key concepts and their logical interrelationship through which problems are posed and solved. A successful performance is defined in terms of particular skills being effectively employed; an understanding of the social and physical world requires the mastery of a range of concepts and recognition of the contexts in which they can be correctly applied. That is what is referred to as the 'logic of the subject matter' – the distinctive concepts and principles through which experience is organized and investigated.

An example of what is meant might be taken from physics. To see the world from the point of view of the physicist would be to see things in terms of atoms and particles, electrons and neutrons, quite abstracted from the ordinary, commonsense way in which the world is normally described in terms of trees and rocks and rivers. Those concepts of physics have enabled scientists for certain purposes to understand the world in a more productive way, both in predicting events and in making new artifacts (e.g. the television). Furthermore, these concepts constitute a pattern of explanations that are logically interconnected in a mathematically tight way. The explanations that they offer are given in rather abstract formulas. To learn physics would be to have gradually mastered these concepts and to have entered into a form of discourse defined by them. That discourse gives a particular way of seeing the world and of identifying 'objects' of a peculiar sort (atoms) which enable causal explanations and predictions within the world of ordinary common sense.

Physics provides the most abstract example. But examples could be given from any type of discourse. One cannot, for example, describe the world from a Christian angle without mastering at some level a particular form of discourse that is characterized by such concepts (and their interrelationship) as 'God', 'worship', 'sin', 'redemption', 'prayer', 'sacrament'. They constitute the 'logical structure' of that particular way of describing and understanding experience.

Furthermore, these abstract and theoretical conceptual frameworks – these logical constructions of reality – have evolved over time and through criticism. They are a human achievement. They 'are themselves experience – they are that of the race. They embody the cumulative outcome of the efforts, the strivings, and successes of the human race generation after generation' (CC, p. 129). They constitute a more objective, explanatory system of thinking that transcends the 'here and now' of each person and strives after universality of explanation. And that achievement comes from generations of researchers, philosophers and academics of different disciplines as they reconceptualize how we describe the world in order to obtain greater explanatory power. That reconceptualizing takes place in order to accommodate awkward facts that fail to fit in with previous theoretical accounts; it takes place through ongoing criticisms within the scientific and other communities. And it is carved up into different subject matters, mastered by specialist experts – custodians, as it were, of these distinctive forms of knowledge.

For purposes of transmission, these forms of knowledge are packaged into discrete subjects, and within these there are textbooks that introduce the learner to the key concepts, modes of inquiry and methods of verification peculiar to these different subjects. But each such subject is but a selection from a complex inheritance of human achievement over the generations, and organized in a way that will be useful for future growth.

Bringing the two together: the teacher and the curriculum

The main task of the teacher is to make the connections between these two worlds:

> first, the narrow but personal world of the child against the impersonal but infinitely extended world of space and time; second, the unity, the single wholeheartedness of the child's life, and the specializations and divisions of the curriculum; third, the practical and emotional bonds of child life and an abstract principle of logical classification and arrangement.
>
> (CC, pp. 126–7, but with this author's reversal of the last two phrases)

The different subject matters embody the evolved knowledge of the human race, as opposed to the immediate and relative knowledge of the individual or small group of individuals. But

> the child and the curriculum are simply two limits which define a single process. Just as two points define a straight line, so the present standpoint of the child and the facts and truths of studies define instruction. It is a continuous reconstruction, moving from the child's present experience out into that represented by the organized bodies of truth that we call studies.
>
> (CC, p. 129)

The educational process creates and maintains the interaction between the two. In so doing, it ensures a constant reconstruction of the child's experience, rather than a denial of the earlier, more childlike experience. But in enabling this interaction and reconstruction, the accumulated knowledge of the human race, having grown through shared experience and having withstood the test of time, helps the teacher to interpret the present interests and experiences of the learner. In so interpreting, in seeing the significance and the promise of those interests, the teacher is thereby able to guide the learner and to help him or her to further those interests and to open up the mind to further and deeper understandings. Learners' attempts to understand the physical and social world in which they live have been anticipated in others' attempts to understand, and thus the learners can benefit from the formulation of those others' experiences. The systematized experience of the 'adult mind' helps in the interpretation of the child's mind, and shows how it might do better what it is trying to do (with more powerful understanding, greater enjoyment, greater ability to perform). The formulated knowledge of the adult mind provides both interpretation and guidance.

Therefore, the interests of the learner, having reached a certain level of understanding, must not be treated as completed achievements, the end of the road, as it were. Rather are they part of living, to be understood as ongoing activities that open up yet further possibilities of knowing, creating and expressing. And the teacher, mediating what others have said and done (within the sciences, the arts and the humanities), enables that interest to progress to further heights of understanding and capability.

To understand this, one needs to see how, for example, the abstractions of mathematical formulas have grown out of what Dewey refers to, in *The Child and the Curriculum*, as 'the child's present crude impulses in counting, measuring, and arranging things in rhythmic series' (p. 134). The abstractions of advanced theory in mathematics or science may seem so remote from 'the child's present crude impulses' as to have no real connection. But historically there is a connection. Consequently, it is important once again to reconnect, first, if those abstractions are to be understood; second, if the possibilities inherent in those impulses (or their expression in various interests) are to be realized.

Bruner

It may help, in the attempt to understand this, to refer once again to the work of Jerome Bruner. In *The Process of Education*, Bruner (1960) shows how the curriculum should arise from a partnership of the physicists, the chemists, the biologists, and so on, on the one hand, and the teachers, on the other. The former are able to identify the key ideas or concepts that are central to their distinctive disciplines – what it means to think and to see things from a distinctively physicist's, or chemist's, or biologist's point of view. What are the key organizing principles and concepts? The teachers, on the other hand, the experts in pedagogy, have the job of translating such abstract ideas into a mode of representation that, though doing justice to those ideas, is within the grasp of the young learner. The curriculum is essentially 'spiral' – a constant revisiting of these same key ideas or concepts but at a higher level of representation. The example given is that of the child on the seesaw. At first the child grasps the concept of leverage enactively, operating successfully on the seesaw through shifting the balance of weight, etc. Subsequently, the child is able to envisage beforehand, and away from the seesaw itself, how it works; he is capable of an 'iconic mode of representation'. Eventually, he is able to express the principles that lie behind the operation of the seesaw. He is entering into the stage of symbolic representation. Those principles can be expressed more mathematically and abstractly. Hence, the same idea is re-enacted but in different ways, so that one can see the relationship between the child's thoughts and the thoughts of the expert mathematician; in the words of Dewey already quoted, 'the child and the curriculum are simply two limits which define a single process'.

To explain this, Dewey provides the analogy of the map:

We may compare the difference between the logical and the psychological to the difference between the notes which an explorer makes in a new country, blazing a trail and finding his way along as best he may, and the finished map that is constructed after the country has been thoroughly explored.

(CC, p. 136)

The map puts together, in a necessarily abstract way (that is, abstracted from the actual descriptions of the terrain by particular people), the different accounts. It relates them together in a single whole. It relates one explorer's experience with the experiences of other explorers. Furthermore, such a map could have been devised otherwise if it were meant to serve different purposes – emphasizing roads rather than railways, different kinds of plant life rather than routes from one place to another. What it certainly is not is a substitute for personal experience itself, to which, nonetheless, given particular interests and purposes, it has to be related. Rather does the map put to the aid of the traveler the wisdom gained from previous travels. It acts as a guide. It saves the traveler from getting lost. It quickens the journey. It shows the route. It prepares the traveler for what might be observed. Similarly, the bodies or forms of knowledge we have inherited should be seen, according to Dewey, as completed maps of the terrain, and, as such, bringing to the ponderings and inquiries of the young learner guides as to the most profitable routes to take. It is the job of the teacher to make these connections. The expertise of the teacher, therefore, lies both in a good grasp of the map – of the subject matter as formulated by the knowledge experts – and, at the same time, in the ability to detect in the interests and tendencies of the young learner how that map might provide an interpretation and a guide.

For the teacher to do this, the subject matter has to be 'psychologized' – that is, reconceptualized in such a way that it can provide a relevant map for those struggling to understand while not distorting the meaning of the abstract theories as formulated by the experts. The subject matter has to be so written as to be accessible to the learner in a way that links to his or her dominant interests and yet that respects the logical structure of the distinct bodies of knowledge. Too often the textbooks (and the teachers who follow the textbooks) fail in this. They provide synopses of the theory while failing to translate that theory into a simple enough map for the interpretation and the guidance of the active thinking and doing of the young learner.

Therefore, the theories, the subject matter of study, the accumulated bodies of knowledge, which explain the social and physical worlds and which are the basis of further research and scholarship, have two aspects. Each such subject is a self-contained theoretical account which is the basis for further inquiry and knowledge, entrusted to scientists, mathematicians, historians, and so. But each subject is also a way that, if properly put across, helps the young learner to understand more effectively the world in which he or she lives. The job of the teacher, therefore, is not to join the ranks of the scientists and the historians in developing theory. Nor is it to transmit that theory as such. Rather, it is to find ways in which this theoretical framework might be translated into a form that illuminates the active engagements of the young people at different stages of understanding and performing. How, the teacher will ask, can the subject become a vital part of the learner's experience?

Dewey frequently worked through examples, and there are several examples of what he meant in *School and Society*, taken from his experience in the University Laboratory School of which he was the director. Perhaps it would be useful if this book, too, 'psychologized' what has been said through examples: one from Dewey, a second from Jerome Bruner's social studies course and a third through an important curriculum development in science to which Dewey would surely have given his blessing, had he been alive, and a fourth through the humanities.

Dewey speaks of young learners being engaged in sewing and weaving – activities that make greater or lesser demands on their interests depending on the level they are at. But the task led on, when properly directed, first, to an understanding of these activities within a broader social and historical significance of them ('In connection with these occupations the historical development of man is recapitulated', SS, p. 92). It led on, second, to an understanding of the technology that was created for the turning of raw materials into cloth and then into clothes.

In more recent times we have seen how Bruner achieved this so well with his 'Man: a course of study', building on the basic interests (practical though they might be) in language, socializing, growing up, myth making or storytelling, and making things (through using tools) to study what it means to be human, how we became so and how we might become more so. What guided these explorations of those characteristics that made us distinctively human were the works of anthropologists, social psychologists, sociolinguists, historians, and so on. The active learning of the young people was enhanced by the teachers in the light of what was known from the subject experts. It was taken on to a different level and opened up to further understanding and inquiry (Bruner, 1966).

Recent reforms in the science curriculum leading to the General Certificate of Secondary Education (GCSE) in England and Wales have reacted to the problem of so many young people failing to be interested in science education, or to progress very far, by developing a suite of 'twenty-first-century science' courses that endeavor to link, in Dewey's words, 'the child to the curriculum'. The aim is to ensure that everyone (not just budding scientists) obtains a good grasp of those scientific concepts that enable them to understand the world in which they live and the issues that impact on the quality of their personal or their community's lives. Thus, basic areas of human living in which the young people, given the opportunity, are deeply interested, such as keeping healthy, using and misusing drugs, avoiding disease, protecting the environment, are explored actively, but guided by the concepts and principles afforded by science. 'Keeping healthy' requires understanding the kind of food that provides the energy, the protection against disease, and the strength necessary for living, or for engaging in different kinds of activity. But what we learn from science – about proteins, vitamins of various kinds, calories, metabolism – enables that interest to be pursued to a more empowering and interesting level, and, where the interest reaches beyond the immediate, into quite theoretical chemistry and biology. The suite of courses caters both for the general interest, pursued through activities, and for those who develop an interest in the deeper theoretical framework.

Another example that would have gained Dewey's approval is that of the Humanities Curriculum Project, established in 1967 by Lawrence Stenhouse at the University of East Anglia in England (see Stenhouse, 1975). The humanities were seen as that area of the curriculum where the concerns of young people (for example, relationships between the sexes, racism, use of violence, relations with authority, injustices of various kinds) could become the focus of exploration but in the light of evidence drawn from drama, literature, poetry, history, theology, science, anthropology, and so on. The matching of the two – the concerns of the students and the 'public knowledge and experience' embodied in the culture we have inherited – took place in the critical but supportive framework of group discussion. The art and the skill of the teacher lay in the management of that exploration.

Discipline

Part of the curriculum development linked to the learner's development is the discipline associated with it. The concept of 'discipline' too often conjures up an image of young people being forced into a form of conduct not to their liking. Often one hears the view that more discipline is required in school or that young people are undisciplined. Discipline is often seen as something imposed from outside by the teacher, say, and enforced through punishment. This is particularly the case where the learner is reluctant – not seeing the point or the interest in the subject matter of the curriculum. If there is no connection between what is taught and what he or she is interested in, then 'discipline' is required to force the learner to take an interest in the subject.

To be disciplined means to be subjected to rules that set out the appropriate ways of proceeding. A thinker is disciplined where he or she adheres closely to the rules of logic or the rules appropriate to the subject being studied. An athlete is disciplined where he or she sticks to a training regime – exercise and food – that will ensure good performance on the track. Someone who is keen to find something out will be self-disciplined – will take the appropriate steps to get the evidence, to ask for expert help, to test out the possible solutions. He or she will resist the temptation to quit, will overcome the many irritations and obstacles that crop up. 'Discipline' therefore refers to sticking to the rules which, if followed, will most likely lead to the intended objective. To be deeply interested in some activity will impose its own discipline, though at times, when the learner feels disheartened, that disciplined approach might need reinforcement and encouragement.

This connection between pursuing an interest and being disciplined is developed fully in Chapter 10 of *Democracy and Education*. The self-discipline that is required to follow an interest, especially when things get difficult, can be developed with help. One can be trained to be more disciplined – to clarify the end and the means to attain that end, to deal with distractions, to master the resources and the skills needed to persevere with the enterprise. We quite rightly talk of a person being trained in a particular discipline – that is, in a way of inquiring.

Above all, however, Dewey sees the development of discipline to arise through joint and cooperative activities, the end of which is of social significance. He saw that the value of traditional family activities, which once upon a time young people were obliged to share in, lay not only in the learning that took place but also in the moral training that such activities afforded. Shared activities required cooperation, reciprocal support, mutual obligations, loyalty to the team, and thus the discipline necessary for working with others. There was no opting out. Everyone had a part to play, and not to play that part would let the team down. There would be the kind of moral force that created the necessary discipline.

Dewey, therefore, remained highly critical of those whose predominant notion of discipline was that of externally imposed sanctions, making the learners toe the line, reluctant though they might be. But such remains a feature of education, so called, where the connection between the logical structure of the subject matter that is transmitted makes little connection with the activity and interests of the learner that that subject matter is meant to illuminate.

Kilpatrick and the project method

An enthusiastic disciple of Dewey thought he had the answer, namely the 'project method'.

William Heard Kilpatrick was a junior colleague of Dewey at Teachers College, Columbia University. He succeeded Dewey as professor of philosophy of education in 1918 and he remained in that post until 1938. As Ryan says, 'as the long time head of the foundations of education department, [Kilpatrick] imparted a decidedly Deweyan stamp to the compulsory courses in the philosophy and sociology of education' (1995, p. 162). He keenly supported Dewey's idea of the ideal school being a regime of purposeful activity. Lawrence Cremin's (1954) book on Teachers College gives a detailed account of this period. Kilpatrick put into practice what he saw as being Dewey's philosophy of education. And the 'Kilpatrick Discussion Group' attracted those who were interested in Dewey's ideas – including Dewey himself. As Ryan says, quoting Cremin,

> The three basic themes that he clung to through thick and thin were Deweyan enough: 'that everything about the schools should prepare the child for a preferred kind of social living; that method should always include purposeful activity; and that the curriculum should consist of what is useful in the present rather than what is to be used in the future'.
>
> (1995, p. 162)

The 'project' would be, according to Kilpatrick, the way of doing this, and thereby of reconciling the impulses or interests of the learner, on the one hand, with, on the other, the knowledge that would enable the learner to pursue those interests. In other words, the 'project' would bridge the gap between the psychological nature of the child and the logical structure of the subject matter.

The problem of teaching, where the intelligent following of interests is central to the educative process, lies chiefly in the choosing of those activities that connect with the concerns and impulses of young people, while at the same time leading on to further interests and further insights. This, at least on the surface, is doubly difficult where the classes are large and contain individuals who might have a wide range of interests. (It should be pointed out that the 'experimental' or 'laboratory' school directed by Dewey in Chicago had a very generous staff : pupil ratio.) And it may be the case that the educational vision of Dewey (and also of Bruner and Stenhouse) can rarely be fully realized in practice. But that in no way invalidates the analysis, or indeed the ideal to which the practice might, in different degrees, approximate.

The answer, therefore, to the practical problems would seem to have been as follows.

First, there is a need to select activities that are not idiosyncratic, but are of general interest; they are perceived to be 'useful in the present', not simply to be used in the future. And they require 'purposeful activity'. An obvious example would be activities concerned with healthy living: choice of food, cooking, exercise. Activities associated with healthy living can be developed to various levels of sophistication, demanding ever more explanatory accounts, the testing of hunches, the sharing of views. The teacher, being aware of the relevant nutritional concepts and knowledge, would be able to give advice on and subtly direct the purposeful activity.

Second, activities that are shared and demand cooperation enhance further the interest, and they create a discipline that otherwise would be lacking. They 'prepared the child for a preferred kind of social living'. Therefore, the school should provide greater opportunities for cooperative work, for social interaction, and for engagement in activities that are deeply connected with the very lives of the young people.

The practical way of doing this would be to identify a suitable project. Kilpatrick saw that this could be achieved through the selection of projects that demanded cooperation among the learners. Where a child is purposefully engaged in a task, he or she would be expected to gain a high degree of skill and understanding, which would produce knowledge that would be permanent. There would be pleasure in school work, enthusiasm for further projects, and a more favorable attitude to social agencies generally. Indeed, his belief was that such active, cooperative project work would produce 'better citizens, alert, able to think and act, too intelligently critical to be easily hoodwinked by politicians or patent-medicines, self-reliant, ready of adaptation to the new social conditions that impend' (Kilpatrick, 1918, p. 334).

In introducing the account of 'an experiment with a project curriculum', Kilpatrick argued that the aims of the school were not the 'conventional knowledge or skills'. The starting point was 'the actual present life of the boys and girls themselves, with all their interests and desires, good and bad'; the first step was 'to help guide these children to choose the most interesting and fruitful parts of this life as the content of their school activity'; and the consequent aims were

> first to help the boys and girls to do better than they would otherwise do the precise things they had chosen, and second, by means of the experience of choosing and through the experience of the more effectual activity to broaden the outlook of the boys and girls as to what they might further choose and then help them better effect those choices.
>
> (Kilpatrick's introduction to Collings, 1923)

It was the belief of Kilpatrick and those who followed him (and there were many during those early decades of the twentieth century) that if children followed such projects and engaged in purposeful activities arising from interests shared by others, their outlook would be 'broadened': they would be led to the understandings and knowledge (the formally constructed bodies of knowledge) that would help them pursue those interests and activities. They would become 'too intelligently critical to be easily hoodwinked by politicians or patent-medicines'.

However, Kilpatrick, admirer and follower of Dewey though he was, lacked the subtlety of Dewey's account. A significant aspect of Dewey's analysis and advocacy of the learner's interests as the starting point and the determinant of the curriculum (and a surprising aspect, given how Dewey has been pilloried by his critics) is, first, his identification of 'interests' with those dispositions and impulses that have the potential for further development and for further inquiry; and second, the direction that the teacher is expected to give to such developing interests in the light of the public knowledge that is relevant to the enhancement of those interests. It is easy to see how Kilpatrick's practical interpretation of Dewey's principles, addressed to generations of trainee teachers, might well have led to the subsequent attack on Dewey's influence. Dewey would not have agreed with Kilpatrick's claim that 'the curriculum [was] continuously made on the spot' (introduction to Collings, 1923) or with Smith et al. (1957, p. 271): 'The interests and purposes of children determine the educational program – what is taught, when it is taught, and the order in which it is taught.' For Dewey, the logical structure of public knowledge, the product of others' inquiries and of their pursuit of related interests in a disciplined way, was, through the agency of the teacher, food, as it were, for the development of those interests. What we crudely call subjects contained the logical structure of knowledge, as that had been constructed by the 'human race', which helped shape the 'purposive activity' of the learner. This directing influence of the teacher was neglected by Kilpatrick's advocacy, in the name of Dewey, of the project method.

Conclusion

The distinction between the psychological and the logical aspects of learning (the phrase is taken from the title of David Hamlyn's influential 1967 paper) is crucial if we are to understand what it means to learn. And yet it is so frequently ignored. Neglect of that distinction leads to one of two opposing and misleading positions.

On the one hand, the neglect of the logical aspect removes the criteria for what counts as 'having learned X or Y'. It leads to such vacuous statements as that of 'teaching children how to learn', as though learning logarithms, learning to ride a bicycle, learning to count, learning how to pray were the same psychological process. But to learn X depends upon the nature of X, and that needs to be spelled out. In some cases that 'spelling out' will involve setting out the interrelated concepts, the mastery of which defines what it means to have understood something. Learning often entails a struggle to understand, a struggle to grasp these concepts – their definition in terms of other concepts already understood and their application to particular instances. To have understood the idea of a 'cat' is, first, to see it as an animal with four legs, whiskers, semi-wild, of the same 'family' as the tiger; and second, to recognize correctly instances of 'cat' in one's experience. In that struggle to understand, one can be mistaken and one needs to be corrected. Or one may have 'half understood' or 'vaguely understood'.

On the other hand, the neglect of the psychological aspect of learning overemphasizes the logical. It results in the transmission of the subject – the formulae in physics, the 'causes' of historical events, the 'explanations' of climate change – without reference to the mode of understanding and to the purposeful activity of the earner. Such 'learning' gets stuck on as with chewing gum or Sellotape (Scotch tape) – not affecting or transforming in any significant way how the learner sees the physical and social worlds.

Dewey was, unlike so many who claimed to follow in his footsteps, a much more subtle thinker than that. He saw both the psychological and the logical aspects of learning, and his genius lay in the distinctive way in which he saw how they should be brought together. This was developed in his 'theory of inquiry', which was explained in Chapter 3. Dewey escapes, however, the crude criticisms of those who, I suspect, have never read *The Child and the Curriculum, School and Society* or *Democracy and Education*. But in so doing, he falls victim to another sort of criticism, that of the philosophers who find fault with his theory of inquiry and criticize his substitution of 'warranted assertion' for 'the truth'.

Chapter 6

Community and the Individual: Democracy and Ethics

The social nature of experience

The social nature of experience is central to all that Dewey wrote. His social philosophy – the meaning and significance of 'community' and the commitment to democracy – is not something apart from his idea of human experience and development, or from his theory of knowledge and truth, or from his theory of ethics. All these are inter-related so strongly that one cannot really consider one part without reference to the whole. But the key element is the social interaction which shapes experience and which is the basis of moral values. Furthermore, such social interaction, when unfettered and constructive, constitutes 'democracy'. This requires careful explanation.

The foregoing chapters have shown how central to Dewey's philosophy of education was the development and the enrichment of experience, for it is in experiencing the world that the human organism grows; it is through *directed* experience that the growing person is able to make sense of the otherwise puzzling world he or she inhabits and is thereby enabled to act intelligently within it.

That world, however, is one not just of material things but also of other people, who themselves are interacting with the physical world and with each other. The social environment, as much as the material environment, is the context of interaction, adaptation, experimentation and transformation. Indeed, it is more so, because the material world is experienced through the connections already established as a result of social activity.

Such connections already established constitute, for Dewey, the cultural environment. The meanings that are embedded in the experiencing of the physical world are the accumulated results of activities shared with, and inherited from, other people, who themselves have come to attach meaning to these interactions in a particular way. For example, a tool (let us say a scythe) is not *just* a physical object; it has meaning in the sense that its *use* (namely, to cut grass or the harvest) is understood, such use being learned through social activities with other people working in the fields. Indeed, such is the interconnection of the physical with the cultural that Dewey argues:

> Of distinctively human behavior it may be said that the strictly physical environment is so incorporated in a cultural environment that our interactions with the former, the problems that arise with reference to it, and our way of dealing with these problems are profoundly affected by incorporation of the physical environment in the cultural.
>
> (LTI, pp. 42–6)

That cultural environment is embodied in the tools we use, the institutions we belong to, the inherited ways of relating to other people, the art forms that surround us. By belonging to social groups (family, village, worshipping community) one internalizes a set of meanings that transforms physical experience from something that one would otherwise react to merely physically (as one blinks when hit in the eye or says 'ouch' when stumbling over a piece of machinery) into something that has a shared meaning, a shared way of connecting experiences that have a purpose within the social group's activities. Furthermore, that internalization of cultural meaning need not (indeed, rarely may be) a conscious process.

That cultural inheritance is registered particularly in the language that the child acquires. That language in turn is acquired (that is, particular noises have meaning and thus become more than a lot of noises) because it is associated with a shared activity, in which it has its roots, as Dewey illustrates in several places (see, for example, DE, p. 15, where he describes the acquisition of the meaning of 'hat' by a young child through the activity of putting on a hat when going for a walk). The interaction, therefore, is not just with the material world, not just with other people in shared activity, but also with the 'signs' of experience and of further activity.

I use the word 'signs' because of its specific meaning within the theory of meaning associated with the philosophy of pragmatism, although, surprisingly, Dewey does not use this particular terminology. But in the interactions between the growing person and the signs that constitute language, although they arise from shared activity, those very signs will themselves be interpreted in the light of the person's own experience. In other words, contrary to what is often assumed, one would not be able to talk of *the* meaning of a particular word (say, 'hat'). The meaning is itself constantly being transformed in the social interactions with which it is associated. It has several changing and interconnected usages, and also different connotations for different people, who associate it with different social experiences.

Therefore, at no time does that world, especially the social understanding of that world, stand still. One can never say one has finally grasped all the connections there are to be made sense of, or that one has 'fully understood' the meaning of what is said or written. The interactions on the social level do themselves transform the environment yet further, requiring a further renewal of how that new social world is to be understood. Everything is in a state of flux. In a sense, as with Heraclitus, Dewey could be said to believe that you can never step in the same river twice.

Importance of community

In *Democracy and Education*, therefore, Dewey refers to 'education' as a 'social function, securing direction and development in the immature through their participation in the life of the group to which they belong' (DE, p. 81). 'The life of the group' constitutes (more or less) a community. Dewey, without giving a definition, hints at what he means by 'community', and why 'community' is crucial to his idea of education (DE, pp. 4–5). Thus, as he argues, people can live closely together (let us say, in a neighborhood) without there being any real communication or reciprocity. There may be forms of interaction, for example in the provision of services for payment, without there being shared aims, values and beliefs. Indeed, because of social and economic arrangements, the machinery of public and private services might be orchestrated to serve efficiently some common goal, while the individuals providing and receiving such services might not constitute a 'community'. For that to be the case, there would need to be shared perceptions of the purposes that those different activities serve, communication between the members of the social group, and responsiveness to the ideas and proposals communicated.

> Men live in a community in virtue of the things which they have in common. What they must have in common in order to form a community or society are aims, beliefs, aspirations, knowledge – a common understanding – likemindedness as the sociologists say.
>
> (DE, p. 4)

Education would, therefore, be different for different communities with different economic bases – for example, a rural farming community as distinct from an urban one. Furthermore, what a community has in common would also change as the wider social, economic and cultural climate changed. Education should be geared to create that greater sense of community and the capacities of the members of it to work together, through full and free association, in responding to such changes.

Such communication and responsiveness do not entail consensus – far from it. The benefits and strengths of a community lie in the communication of differences, and thereby in the growth of that community through the seriousness with which those differences are addressed and modified.

Community in this sense can exist (or not exist) at different levels: those of the family, neighborhood, school or country. They can exist in different kinds of space: the physical space of classroom or street, or the wider distances covered by correspondence between like-minded people. No doubt Dewey would acknowledge as 'communities' those participating in 'organic online communities' afforded by websites and email.

It would be quite possible for community to exist, say, at neighborhood level, but not at the neighborhood school – or vice versa. Hence, for Dewey it was important to create a community within the school where, through reciprocity of relationships and shared aims and values, teachers and students would grow through sharing experiences, through acquiring the virtues of working with others supportively yet critically, and through respecting and learning to understand and benefit from the beliefs of other people. What constitutes a community would seem to be, for Dewey, not sameness of opinion but reciprocal respect, some shared values and the readiness to listen to and to learn from others. These seem to be the necessary conditions for genuine communication, and communication is at the heart of learning and personal growth.

In simple societies, 'society' and 'community' might be considered as synonymous. Survival required common purposes and the virtues essential to interdependent living. The economic base of living required shared aims and understandings. 'Education' of the next generation would require the handing on of skills and values that served the common good, as that was perceived.

Modern society, however, can no longer depend upon such informal ways of inducting the next generation into the skills and values of society. The New York within which Dewey wrote *Democracy and Education* presented a very different sort of society: one that depended upon a range of different economic activities, which would lead to many individuals and groups being alienated and marginalized, and which encompassed people from widely different religious and cultural backgrounds. In such a potentially disintegrating society, as each pursued his or her own goal at the expense of others or as subgroups (subcommunities) split from each other, often in hostile circumstances, the school needed to take on a much more active role. That role was twofold. First, the school would need to enhance, if not create, the community within its own walls. Second, such a school community would need to prepare its students to extend the idea of community within its neighborhood and further afield. Again, by community here is meant a group that shares the very values through which communication and therefore reciprocal learning can take place, and where relationships are not those of power enforcement.

For Dewey, therefore, there is a close, logical link between educating, communicating, being in a community, and personal growth. From within such a community the sharing of aims and ideas would lead to further understanding of the community itself, leading to further development. The community would be this group of people intercommunicating, thereby constantly changing its social character as a result of this communication. The very antithesis of community (and of personal growth within such communities) would be the autocratic or despotic society, whose very character is built on the stifling of communication. Ideas are discouraged, received assumptions unchallenged, external people or societies ignored or treated with hostility.

Hence, a greater variety of peoples within the community (of different ethnicities, political values, religious convictions) should enrich the process of communication, thereby enhancing personal growth – that is, the openness to further ideas, the critical questioning of received assumptions, the readiness to enrich one's own understandings through their being tested in experience and in the critical engagement with others. Schools should be such communities *par excellence*, but in fact too often their hierarchical and autocratic nature inhibits that sharing of aims and experiences. The learner is expected to receive what the teacher transmits without the opportunity to question or to internalize that which is transmitted.

Democratic conditions of growth

It is easy to see, following the central place of communication in the educational experience of the learner, the connection between 'education' and 'democracy'. Genuine communication requires reciprocity and mutual respect. Each person, in one sense, is of equal value in the communicative process, since each has an opinion or viewpoint that is worthy of serious treatment. Each brings a different set of experiences to our understanding of a situation. Each person is capable, in the light of sharing experiences and listening to others' criticisms and accounts of experience, to reorganize how he or she sees things, thereby affecting that person's further contribution to the common experience and understanding. The basis, then, of a democratic society (whatever its specific formal structure for expressing and reinforcing this may be) is mutual respect and shared purposes – and the 'freedom of action', backed up by the 'freed capacity of thought'.

Fundamental to Dewey's commitment to such mutual respect as a basis for democratic communities was his 'faith in the common man' and in the human community that the common man could create and be enriched by. Thus, he argues in his short book *A Common Faith* that the unity aspired to in religion could be achieved in intelligently self-conscious commitment to the human community.

Therein, however, lies a particular understanding of democracy. It is the kind of community in which there is maximum participation in the deliberations about all matters that affect the lives of those within the community, and in the decisions that arise out of those deliberations. And such maximum participation is desirable not because it is likely to be more efficient but because it is a condition of human flourishing. Any other conception of democracy fails to do justice to the very basis of democracy, namely the dignity of all people in shaping their lives through their sharing and deliberations over their respective experiences and views of the world.

This is contrasted by Dewey with Aristotle's notion of democracy, which divides people in society between those who work for the economic context in which others can devote their time to engage in ethical and political discussion. There is a need to extend the elitist notion not only to include all but also to take seriously the different experiences of all (including the conditions of the workers and of industry) in order to make sense of experience. It is contrasted, also, with that form of democracy that merely allocates to the governed the power to reject its representatives once every four or so years if they have failed in their duties.

This ideal rested on a

> faith in the capacity of human beings for intelligent judgment and action if proper conditions are furnished, [a faith] so deeply embedded in the methods which are intrinsic to democracy that when a professed democrat denies the faith he convicts himself of treachery to his profession.
>
> (Dewey, 1939, 'Creative democracy: the task before us', quoted in Westbrook, 1991, p. xv)

In order to achieve this, the school should be open to the rich variety of experiences that young people bring with them to school and that in the hierarchical context of the traditional school too often get neglected as insignificant. But it is precisely those experiences that need education. The link between education and democracy is exactly that: the creation of a space where the experiences of each and every learner would be respected and become the object of the communicative process. The school as a community would find a space for the voice of the learners as they articulated their experiences, shared them with others in the community, learned from the criticisms and articulations of others and contributed to the common understanding of the school and of the world outside the school.

The alternative would be, and is, a system of learning where bodies of knowledge are transmitted and learned but where such transmitted knowledge, ignoring the experience of the learners, generally leaves them, in matters that are important for them, where they were. That knowledge is stuck on, as it were – and it soon becomes unstuck, leaving little trace of its ever having been there at all.

Democracy, therefore, is at the centre of Dewey's moral conception of education (a secular realization of this kingdom of God on earth) and is deeper and wider than any political arrangement. Democracy is a deep and active communication between individuals. It welcomes and sustains diversity of experience and background. It reflects the constant attempt to break down the barriers that inhibit communication – those of social class, racial stereotyping or selective schooling. Any such separateness impoverishes the experience of all. It blocks off the experiences of others from which one's own experience would be enriched. The privately educated upper-class student is impoverished by the lack of understanding about how less privileged people live – and that has so often been the cause no doubt of the unwise policies and decisions of a ruling elite. One is reminded of Tawney's statement in his book *Equality*:

> [I]n spite of their varying character and capacities, men possess in their common humanity a quality which is worth cultivating and ... a community is most likely to make the most of that quality if it takes it into account in planning its economic organisation and social institutions – if it stresses lightly differences of wealth and birth and social position, and establishes on firm foundations institutions which meet common needs, and are a source of common enlightenment and common enjoyment.
>
> (1938, pp. 55–6)

The solution, according to Tawney, in words that could have been Dewey's, is a community with 'a common culture, because, without it, it is not a community at all' (ibid., p. 17).

Furthermore, such a democratic concept of education finds no room for education as a form of social engineering. Education has no end beyond the fruitful extension or enlightenment of the experienced life of the learner, which essentially takes place within communities and needs to take into account the flourishing of those communities. The premise is that all individuals are equally important and that the experiences of each are relevant to the experiences of the whole. Equality of respect is central.

Of course, in another sense each is not equal. The teacher is (or should be) in possession of a wider experience and of the knowledge (the selection from what the community has inherited from past generations) that will widen the opportunity for further fruitful experience. But that particular superiority of the teacher is to serve the growing awareness of the young learner as he or she is striving to make sense of experience, and to put that experience to living more fruitfully in the future. The teacher's job is to serve the learner. The learners' ends or purposes (not those of the teacher) should shape the teaching and learning, those ends being to participate in the deliberations and decisions, as far as is possible, that affect the lives of everyone.

Schools as communities

Why schools? The answer is twofold.

First, Dewey saw education as 'a social function, securing direction and development in the immature through their participation in the life of the group to which they belong' (DE, p. 81). Left entirely to themselves, young children would not be able to organize its experiences and make the connections in order to anticipate or deal with future experiences. There are limits to how often a child can be allowed to burn his or her fingers. A lot has to be learned before there can be any independent living – the use of tools, for example. In less complicated societies that education could take place informally.

One became part of an active community, first through the family, then through the wider village community. From parents one would see and internalize the experiences of homemaking and of farming. One would learn by doing and imitating.

However, that 'securing of direction and development' had become too complicated for such informal educating to take place. The accumulation of past experiences had needed to be formulated in books and artifacts, with a view to short-circuiting the period needed to benefit from such experiences. Schools were established to facilitate that – to bring together the formulated experience of the past and the unformulated experiences of the present with a view to enriching those experiences, and ensuring that, in the light of the past, they would facilitate future action. As Dewey put it,

> Roughly speaking, [schools] come into existence when social traditions are so complex that a considerable part of the social store is committed to writing and transmitted through written symbols ... As soon as a community depends to any considerable extent upon what lies beyond its own territory and its own immediate generation, it must rely upon the set agency of schools to insure adequate transmission of all its resources ... Hence, a special mode of intercourse is instituted, the school, to care for such matters.
>
> (DE, p. 19)

And, later, talking of that interaction between other learners, and between those learners and past generations, made possible by the community of the school, Dewey says of the school that '[p]urposive education or schooling should present such an environment that this interaction will effect acquisition of those meanings which are so important that they become, in turn, instruments of further learnings' (DE, p. 274). However, the value of that exposure to the accumulated wisdom of the past lay in the extent to which it illuminated and transformed the present experiencing, and enabled the young learner to cope with the changes that had not been anticipated in the past. There is a constant need for society, like all social groups, to renew itself by being open to new ideas and to changing needs and possibilities.

Of course, such experiencing would itself be differently interpreted by different students, who would bring to school different
backgrounds and understandings. And Dewey was tough in his con-
demnation of uniformity, or indeed of the simple classification of
young people into a few types. Plato was particularly castigated for his
division of learners into three types:

> In some individuals, appetites naturally dominate; they are assigned
> to the laboring or trading class, which expresses and supplies human
> wants. Others reveal, upon education, that over and above appetites,
> they have a generous, outgoing, assertively courageous disposition.
> They become the citizen-subjects of the state, its defenders in war, its
> internal guardians in peace. But their limit is fixed by their lack of
> reason, which is a capacity to grasp the universal. Those who possess
> this are capable of the highest kind of education – and become in
> time the legislators of the state – for laws are the universal which
> control the particulars of experience.
>
> (DE, p. 90)

This rigid division between types of children failed to do justice to
the massive variety in terms of interests, motivation, aptitude and
stages of growth. It failed to do justice to the unique nature of each
individual. By so categorizing young people, it failed to recognize
their distinctive educational needs. And yet, as is shown in the final
chapter of this book, such a threefold classification has persisted and
shapes the policy of education, certainly in England.

School, then, is the agent for the community to make available
what it, or the larger society and culture of which it is part, has accomplished. Hence, it is a matter not of what some pedagogues think is
best for their pupils but of what society wants for all its citizens if they
are to participate intelligently and actively in their common interests.
What is made accessible would be linked to the march of events and
thus to the changes that have transformed society (for example, the
shift from home industry with particular relationships to factories,
and to wider and global communities). Schools *qua* communities
have to do two things. First, they have to compensate for the lack of
immediacy in the experience of that which is to be understood (links

have to be made by the teacher between the present experiences of the young person and the 'making sense' of those experiences as that is embedded within the inherited culture). Second, they have to prepare the young learners to anticipate and to adapt positively to the kinds of situations they are likely to encounter. Such preparation could not be managed in the purely informal setting of the informal, small community.

The second, and connected, reason for there being schools is that, in being communities themselves, they (ideally) embody the moral virtues and qualities of the wider community to which the young person potentially belongs and in which he or she is to be an active participant. 'The school must itself be a community life in all that that implies' (DE, p. 358). The school *community*, if that is what it is, is essentially a moral community in which, through participation, the young person grows as a moral person, learns how to interact fruitfully with other people, benefits from the different ways of understanding experience, learns how to work cooperatively with others for the good of the whole, builds up a common experience, welcomes through work and play the close association with others, and is continuous with the wider community outside the school.

The importance of this moral aspect of schooling was enhanced by the social changes that Dewey was witnessing. Society was becoming less homogeneous as a result of the immigration of many peoples of different ethnicities, different religions and different cultures. A sense of community of the kind that previously might have prevailed could not be taken for granted. The school should be, therefore, a source of integration, not in the sense of creating uniformity and destroying diversity but in the sense of enabling future citizens to understand and to learn from each other, to respect life-views that differed from their own, to respect others even where one disagreed with them, and to work cooperatively with people who had different 'ends-in-view'. Such cooperative endeavor, if engaged in with seriousness and with respect, would be more than a mere toleration of differences. It would be a further factor in the evolution of each person's understanding of experience and capacity to engage in yet further dialogue and cooperative interaction.

Hence, it is not any sort of 'inherited experience', made available by the school, that is important, but that experience which ensures the conditions for democratic living, for only in such conditions is the enrichment of experience assured. Dewey, therefore, is very insistent on the significance of the 'common school' in the promotion of such democracy. As he says,

> School facilities must be secured of such amplitude and efficiency as will in fact and not simply in name discount the effects of economic inequalities, and secure to all the wards of the nation equality of equipment for their future careers. Accomplishment of this end demands not only adequate administrative provision of school facilities, and such supplementation of family resources as will enable youth to take advantage of them, but also such modification of traditional ideals of culture, traditional subjects of study and traditional methods of teaching and discipline as will retain all the youth under educational influences until they are equipped to be masters of their own economic and social careers. The ideal may seem remote of execution, but the democratic ideal of education is a farcical but tragic delusion except as the ideal more and more dominates our public system of education.
>
> (DE, p. 98)

Control of schools: the role of teachers

Schools, therefore, are communities that enable young people to benefit from the 'accumulated wisdom of the race', as they extend their experiences and as they come to adapt to an ever more complex social and economic environment. They are communities that demonstrate how to participate in a community, to contribute to it and to help it to adapt to changes external to the community. The young person acquires the virtues and skills of interaction with the other members, arising from full and free association, despite (or stimulated by) the differences between them.

The teacher is the one who facilitates this development. In so doing, the teacher needs the following knowledge and skills. First, the teacher has to know the child very well, the interests that engage his or her attention and that can be directed to the desirable 'ends-in-view', which are immanent in those interests. Second, the teacher must be knowledgeable of the cultural inheritance (embodied formally in various subject matters) that illuminates and enriches those interests. Third, the teacher is able to link the two through the process of inquiry, helping to identify the problem, to formulate hypotheses, to suggest possible solutions and to test these out in experience. Fourth, the teacher is to coordinate such inquiry among those belonging to the community of young people, respecting the different ways in which the various interests interact and the subject matter is interpreted by these individuals. The teacher is a sort of *primus inter pares* within the community of learners. As such, he or she is the mediator between the public world, embodied in books and artifacts (the wisdom of the race), and the personal world of the learner as he or she endeavors to make sense of experience and to become capable of adapting fruitfully to further experience.

This very special relationship Dewey hints at in his criticism of the method of teaching identified with Herbart, since this ('the pedagogue's view' of teaching through instruction) did not attach sufficient significance to the active interaction of the learner with the environment – the reinterpretation of the subject matter within the learner's existing internalized system of 'making sense' – and with the teacher. 'It slurs over the fact that the environment involves a personal sharing in common experiences' (DE, p. 71). It slurs over, too, the distinctive role of the teacher in this personal sharing:

> The alternative to furnishing ready-made subject-matter and listening to the accuracy with which it is reproduced is not quiescence, but participation, sharing, in an activity. In such shared activity, the teacher is a learner, and the learner is, without knowing it, a teacher – and upon the whole, the less consciousness there is, on either side, of either giving or receiving instruction, the better.
>
> (DE, p. 160)

Such a teacher must be responsible for the overall organization of learning, not someone external to the school. An external person (politician or civil servant) could not have the specific knowledge or the relevant experience to adapt to the particular young people and to their experiences. Such an external person could not be involved in the shared experience and the reciprocal relationship that are essential to teaching. In other words, the teacher should be seen as part of the democratic community with a specific role, namely that of interpreting and responding to the ways in which the child understands experience. That response requires a 'psychologizing' (Dewey's term; see Chapter 5) of the relevant subject matter by the teacher so that its connection to present experience and interests can be seen and so that direction can be given to further experiencing and inquiry. In so doing, the teacher should be given the freedom to make decisions about the curriculum, appropriate learning experiences, methods of discipline, textbooks, etc. – freedom to respond to the learning requirements of the moment, from his or her own expertise in the development of the child, on the one hand, and, on the other, in the 'race-expression which is embodied in that thing we call the Curriculum'. Indeed,

> until the public-school system is organized in such a way that every teacher has some regular and representative way in which he or she can register judgment upon matters of educational importance, with assurance that this judgment will somehow affect the school system, the assertion that the system is not, from the internal stand-point, democratic seems to be justified.
>
> (quoted from an article that appeared in *The Elementary School Teacher*, 1903)

Dewey was scathing about the undemocratic way in which schools were run, and thereby the autocratic treatment of teachers:

> the dictation, in theory at least, of the subject-matter to be taught, to the teacher who is to engage in the actual work of instruction ... [which] meant nothing more than the deliberate restriction of intelligence, the imprisonment of the spirit.
>
> (ibid.)

Such autocracy was out of step with the democratic principles that permeated other areas of public life. And democracy in schools (that is, the freedom to be enjoyed by the learners to explore ideas and by the teachers to exercise judgment) could not be created by the transfer of power from textbook publishers or state assemblies to the school superintendent. That was simply a transfer of power to an autocracy. Democracy is the condition of intellectual freedom of those within the community, and such intellectual freedom applies both to the learners and to the teachers.

Ethics and morals

It might seem strange that Dewey's underlying theory of moral values should be dealt with in this chapter, but ethics, as the philosophical study of morals, could not be isolated from the relation of individuals to the community, or from the close connection that Dewey made between morals and democracy – or, better still, between acting morally and acting democratically.

Morality, in Dewey's account, concerns freedom to pursue our own wants (to seek our own 'ends-in-view'), compatible with others pursuing their own particular objectives – bearing in mind that everyone is actively pursuing their respective wants within a social context in which each is interacting with others. Morality, therefore, concerns the closing of the gap between what we want for ourselves, what others want for themselves and what we want for others. In order to achieve this, moral engagement requires two things.

First, it constitutes *intelligent action,* in the sense of integrating the demands of our different wants; it concerns the assurance of unity and coherence within our lives. For example, we want both to spend the evening at the theater and to finish the paper promised for the morrow; there is a tension between the fulfilling of different wants. Which of these different wants should be given priority? Going to the theater may be seen as a well-deserved relaxation after a stressful week. On the other hand, the paper was *promised.* How much weight should be put on the promising? In such deliberation, one would need to weigh up the consequences, and think especially of the social consequences of not keeping promises, even where the breaking of that particular promise may not have serious consequences. Moral deliberation is about the particular; and no particular situation, with all its complexity, can be adequately covered by appeal to one or two major and universal principles.

Second, morality requires an integration of those wants with the wants of others. Though the theater would be the more attractive choice, this is incompatible with the benefit to the person for whom the paper was written. There is a conflict between goals within the individual and goals within a group of individuals, and these need to be resolved. The conditions of humankind in present society are essentially ones where there is need for constant reciprocal adjustment of individuals to society and within it – hence the importance of democratic community, where such tensions can be resolved and where individuals can be enabled to pursue their separate 'ends-in-view', while adjusting to and learning from others. Therefore, Dewey concludes the chapter in *Reconstruction in Philosophy* entitled 'Reconstruction in moral conceptions' with this link between moral meaning and democracy:

> Democracy has many meanings, but if it has a moral meaning, it is to be found in resolving that the supreme test of all institutions and industrial arrangements shall be the contribution they make to the all-round growth of every member of society.
>
> (RP, p. 186)

The growth of the individual cannot be isolated from that individual's interaction with others, who provide either an obstacle to growth or the conditions for further growth. Those individuals are interacting with greatest advantage to each and all where they take place within a community defined in terms of shared understandings and shared rules for working with each other. Democracy is where those relationships and rules are such as to free each person to pursue his or her own 'ends-in-view', as far as is compatible with the 'ends-in-view' of the other members. And, of course, in seeking or ensuring that compatibility, so that very growth is enhanced, benefiting from the insight gained from others' aspirations and aims.

To understand the meaning that is here being attributed to 'moral', one needs to see what Dewey was arguing against. In his book *Reconstruction in Philosophy*, published in 1920, he speaks critically of traditional philosophical accounts of morality. Ethics (the study of morals and thus of what is good and obligatory) has been mesmerized by the search for the end or goal of all human activity – what all human beings should strive for (holiness, happiness of the greatest number, specific virtues, obedience to the divine laws, universalizability of principles, loyalty to the state, etc.). It assumes a singleness of purpose, a 'final good', that is relevant to all people. But what constitutes that final good is forever, and inevitably, disputed, without any sign of there being a way in which to resolve those disagreements. Morality would thus be a matter of succumbing to prescriptions that initially are external to the learner and that need to be internalized and applied in the appropriate circumstances.

This, however, for Dewey was but another example of the dualism that is incompatible with his notion of the growing organism, whose 'good' or 'end-in-view' is, in a sense, internal to the active organism as it pursues its proper growth, and realizes itself more fully through further growth. Indeed, as he constantly asserts, 'growth itself is the only moral "end"' (RP, p. 177).

To understand this further we need to see how Dewey wished to apply what he saw to have succeeded in science and other areas of life – the experimental method – to moral deliberations. The experimental method, which had been so successful in the sciences, had respected the individual case. Generalizations were acceptable until falsified by the particular experience. In the experimental method, one clarified the problem that had arrested action. One looked at all the circumstances of the problem and thought of a way forward, formulating it as precisely as possible. One then tested out that possible way against experience.

The experimental method enabled a person, puzzled about what to do, to clarify the practical problem, to survey all the conditions that determine what is possible or not possible, to think of possible solutions, to test them out and to observe what happened. If it resolved the problem then it had achieved the individual good, and that was the only good there was to be resolved.

Such flexibility and adaptation to individual circumstances was not, however, typical of philosophical accounts of moral deliberation, in which general principles were appealed to and applied to circumstances that differed a great deal in detail. Appeal to experience, as a way of testing the general principle (did it remove the problem such that one could pursue the activity within the community of individuals?), was seen to be irrelevant. The practical use of morality – its meaning in terms of its having a desirable effect – was not recognized. Traditional ethics saw moral principles as shaping practice rather than as facilitating it – just as theory (prior to the application of the experimental method) shaped our understanding of the physical and social worlds, rather than succumb to the exceptions and singularity of experience. Such philosophical accounts failed to see that moral thinking is practical thinking and arises from specific puzzles about what to do. 'What to do' – the aims to be pursued and the goods to be acquired – could be many, and certainly they differ from person to person.

However, the resolution of a practical problem (what to do) could not take place in a social vacuum. The problem would not be resolved if the tentative solution created yet more problems because one was, as a result, now living at loggerheads with one's neighbor. Hence, the 'solution' opened up yet further experimentation, taking into account the other's perspective. In that way, so it would seem, the pursuit of one's own good, 'through following the pragmatic rule' of seeing the meaning of what one was doing through examining the possible consequences, necessarily required the pursuit of the good of other people – the good of the community of which one was an intrinsic part. Pursuing one's own good (resolving one's own problems, but within the community to which one belonged) meant that there was continual growth, and such growth was the main moral aim and the aim of education.

Many will find such a position unacceptable, for a couple of reasons.

First, whatever the difficulties we have in justifying the external base for our moral obligations (and Dewey exploits those difficulties in arguing that all are misconceived in trying to find just one overriding moral principle), the seeming alternative position, that of personal relativism, also seems unacceptable. We do engage in moral

deliberation and struggle in deciding what to do, and such deliberation and struggle make sense only if there are constraints on what
is permissible, and those constraints are not a matter of arbitrary
choice. Not any behavior is acceptable, even behavior that might be
acceptable to the other members of the group. Furthermore, even the
'moral authorities' within different communities are open to moral
questioning, and such questioning presupposes principles or criteria
of right and wrong to which the questioner feels obliged to submit.

Second, the general position comes up against awkward counter-
examples, which Dewey tries to deal with, although not, according to
his critics, very successfully. Since there are no external criteria for
deciding that a particular action is immoral, the moral character of
the action has to be intrinsic to the formal principles of the human
organism's growth itself – the extent to which (in the words of the idealists who had influenced Dewey) the human organism had realized
its true self. But that 'true self' was essentially the capacity for more
growth – for being able more effectively to adapt to the social and
physical environment and to anticipate and to overcome obstacles
to further growth. However, such a theory of value would not seem
able to exclude the growth that, on other grounds, we would wish to
exclude as grossly immoral. Thus, the petty thief engages in experiences that open up the possibility of an interesting and varied life of
crime; there might well be a considerable growth in all sorts of enriching experiences: the sociological and psychological understanding of
others' motivations and modes of living, the manual skills required
of competent burglars – leadership qualities as his team of successful
thieves is built up, entrepreneurship and enterprise, and finally an
aesthetic appreciation of the art stolen or bought through the profits
of crime. We would, however, wish to argue that the growth was in the
wrong direction, wrongness being judged by criteria disconnected
from the formal characteristics of growth itself.

Dewey's reply to this is, at first sight, far from satisfactory. He said
that growth in a particular direction of this sort retarded 'growth in
general [because it] sets up conditions that shut off the person ...
from the occasions, stimuli, and opportunities for continuing growth
in new directions' (EE, p. 36). And yet what Dewey says is plausible.
It would be difficult to think of thieving or robbery without others

being thwarted in what they saw to be the legitimate pursuit of their particular wants. Such a 'company of thieves' would detract from the solidarity and enrichment of the wider community wherein, with shared understandings and rules of procedure, contributions would be made by all 'to the all-round growth of every member of society'. Some, if not many, would be prevented from, rather than freed to enrich, the growth that is proper to them.

Furthermore, the 'virtues' or dispositions that were intrinsic to such self-realization or growth within a social environment and community and that were spelled out by Dewey were surprisingly like the virtues that we would associate with being moral: perseverance and steadfastness, openness to alternative views, modesty in the proclamation of one's own achievement, sensitivity to the needs and motivations of others, loyalty to the democratic values and the community that maintained them, courage in sticking to what one believed in, humility in the readiness to submit to wiser opinion, honesty in being true to what one believed.

The social interactions that provide the possibility of this virtuous growth take place most effectively within supportive, participative and thus democratic communities. Within the sharing of understandings and general purposes, the individual identifies with the 'virtues' of that community as it is, but, in recognizing tensions and failings within it, nudges that community toward ideals that are embodied, but not yet fully realized, within the life of the community. The society or community, let us say, was democratic, but not as democratic as it might be – participation extending perhaps only to some institutions, not to all (as was the case in schools). In such communities there is no opposition between self-interest, community interest and morality. Indeed, the distinction between morality and intelligent action disappears where morality is seen as 'the intelligent management of life in a society'. One accepts the community's standards but pushes the community gradually to embed the ideals that are intrinsic to being a community and that enhance the free pursuit of what satisfies each person, towards a more complete realization. Duties are tied to the notion of living healthily within a community. But that understanding of community can gradually be extended more and more widely. The search for unity of explanation which lies behind religion can be achieved through 'intelligent self-conscious commitment to the human community'.

Just as the aim of education is the facilitation of growth through the direction of appropriate experience, so the institutional organization of education through schools must aim to create the conditions for such growth, one major condition being that of the democratic community, which alone respects and makes possible the pursuit of individual goods compatible with the goods of all its members.

Part 3

Philosophical Underpinnings

Chapter 7

Pragmatism: Meaning, Truth and Value

Philosophical influences

I referred in Chapter 1 to three powerful intellectual influences on
Dewey's philosophical, and hence educational, thinking: first, the
prevailing evolutionary understanding of human development, arising from Darwin's *Origin of Species* and the subsequent debate; second, neo-Hegelian idealism, especially through the influence of the
Oxford philosopher T.H. Green; and third, the prevailing 'pragmatism', usually associated with Charles Sanders Peirce (a colleague
of Dewey at Johns Hopkins University, although relations between
Dewey and Peirce do not seem to have been warm, and there is little
reference in the works of either to each other).

In what follows, I shall examine each of these separately before
bringing them together in what is intended to be the distinctive philosophical position of Dewey.

Evolutionary theories

Evolution of the human species pointed to the continuity of development from primitive life to the self-conscious life of the human
person. There is a gradual maturing of capacities as species are transformed into ones with greater capacity for adaptation, including the
increase of sensory, and then reflective, capacities. Species, at any
level, can be understood, both in their adaptive function and in their
evolutionary development of capacities, only from a teleological point
of view – striving to reach ends appropriate to their distinctive natures.

Two interesting things follow from this.

The first is that there is no sudden break in essence between beings
at different stages of evolution. Just as we do not attribute a mind or

a soul to a plant or an animal as a separate substance, mysteriously guiding or affecting the material body, neither do we do so to the human organism. People (human organisms) are not two substances (mind and body) joined together, but one substance. 'This philosophy is vouched for by the doctrine of biological development which shows that man is continuous with nature, not an alien entering her processes from without' (DE, p. 285). Here we see the debt of Dewey to the work of Darwin. Indeed, Dewey saw the theory of evolution as having a radical effect on how we should conceptualize the relationship between mind and body – that is, resolve the opposition between the rationalists and the empiricists with their different versions of the mind–body dualism. He concludes his essay 'The influence of Darwinism on philosophy' thus:

> [I]ntellectual progress usually occurs through sheer abandonment of questions together with both of the alternatives which they assume ... Doubtless the greatest dissolvent in contemporary thought of old questions, the greatest precipitant of new methods, new intentions, new methods, new intentions, new problems, is the one effected by the scientific revolution that found its climax in *The Origin of Species*.
>
> (in Capps and Capps, 2005, p. 188)

Cartesian dualism was seen by Dewey as being grossly mistaken. Indeed, it is important to get rid of the idea of 'mind' as a thing – deceived, as we seemingly are, by the use of a noun rather than an adjective. Rather do we need to think of the human organism as having certain advanced capacities that are called mental: the capacity to imagine, to reflect and to remember. Many of the illusions in educational practice are due to this false dualism – for example, 'thinking' separated from 'doing', and theory distinct from, and superior to, practice.

There are remarkable similarities between what Dewey said and what Karl Popper argued in his paper 'Towards an evolutionary theory of knowledge':

> My starting point is a very simple proposition – indeed an almost trivial one – the proposition that animals can know something: that they can have knowledge. For example, a dog can know that his

master returns home, on working days, at 6 p.m. and the behaviour of the dog may give many indications, clear to his friends, that he expects the return of his master at that time. I shall show that, in spite of its triviality, the proposition that animals can know something completely revolutionizes the theory of knowledge as it is widely taught.

(Popper, 1999, p. 58)

This 'revolutionizing of the theory of knowledge' lies in the shift from the spectator view of knowledge (the human mind reflecting or mirroring a world independent of 'the mind') to one in which knowledge lies in the organism's increased capacity to adapt to new situations – to solve problems through constantly revising the expectations (the hypotheses) with which one confronts experience. In that sense, the difference between the dog and the human being is a difference of degree, not one of kind. The quite radical difference between animals and human beings is questioned where 'knowing' is seen to be a way of adapting to the environment in the light of previous experiences and, therefore, where dogs, clearly seen to be so adapting, can be said to know that something is the case.

How 'revolutionary' this is becomes apparent when one considers the standard definition of knowledge, which was set out in A.J. Ayer's *The Problem of Knowledge* but in essence repeated in many other philosophical texts:

I conclude then that the necessary and sufficient condition for knowing that something is the case are first that what one is said to know is true, secondly that one be sure of it, and thirdly that one should have the right to be sure.

(Ayer, 1947, p. 35)

'Knowledge' is thus defined in this way. X knows that 'p', where (1) 'p' is true, (2) X believes strongly that 'p', and (3) X has good grounds for believing that 'p' is true. With regard to (1), there is a world existing independently of my beliefs to which in some way those beliefs either do or do not correspond. With regard to (2), one has a belief or a mental state associated with a feeling of certainty. With regard to (3), 'knowledge' is distinguished from 'mere opinion'; it requires verification, or at least strong evidence, which is logically associated with that kind of knowledge claim. Often this analysis is (though it need not necessarily be) associated with there being solid foundations upon which bodies of knowledge are built (that is, upon what has been conclusively verified or upon what is necessarily presupposed in any knowledge claim, such that the knowledge subsequently constructed is on secure and proven foundations).

What, then, is revolutionary in Popper's view is the shift from the conception of a mental activity, which is reflected in the propositions the mind entertains, which mirrors somehow a world separate from it and which checks out whether that mirror is an accurate picture. Within such a conception, the emphasis is on the theoretical aspect of knowing: the building up of descriptions of the physical and social worlds and of the explanations of why things, so described, happen. In Popper's account there is a radical change from that understanding of 'knowing' to one of an active organism, practically engaged in problem solving, adapting to new situations, and internalizing the solution in anticipation of new and similar problems. Popper's essay, interestingly, is to be found in a collection of essays entitled *Life Is All Problem Solving*.

The main thrust of the argument is reflected in another of his essays found in the same collection, 'On evolutionary epistemology'.

> We learn only through trial and error. Our trials are always our hypotheses. They stem from us, not from the external world. All we learn from the external world is that some of our efforts are mistaken. From the primitive forms of life onwards, from the earliest cells, adaptation is an invention on the part of living creatures.
>
> (Popper, 1999, p. 46)

The second consequence, therefore, of the evolutionary continuity of different species, including the human, is that each organism must be understood teleologically – as actively striving for an end or goal that is immanent within it. To put it in more scholarly terms, each organism has to be understood in terms of final as well as efficient causes – an idea that was anathema to the prevailing tradition of empiricism. Just as the seed of a plant is programmed to become a runner bean or a potato, so the human organism is programmed to make connections between experiences and to build up, as it were, an internal organization of experience that 'gives meaning' to further experiences. The human organism is programmed to construct, not just receive, experiences. Therefore, although Dewey eliminates the mind as a separate substance, he is not left with the body as part of the physical world which can be understood simply in terms of physical causes. He therefore attacks the prevailing 'behaviorism' of J.B. Watson, which, in getting rid of the mind as a separate substance, failed to see the mental qualities that characterize human activity.

It is surprising that despite the similarity between Popper's 'revolutionizing of the theory of knowledge' and Dewey's pragmatic reduction of knowledge to 'warranted assertion', the former makes no reference to the latter.

Idealism

Interestingly, the teleological understanding of organisms, especially the human organism, was interpreted by Dewey within a tradition of Hegelian idealism. It is a tradition to which he was exposed when he went to Johns Hopkins University, mainly through the influence of his mentor, Charles Morris, whom he later followed to the University of Michigan. It would be wrong to see Dewey as a thoroughgoing Hegelian, especially as he came to develop his own distinctive kind of pragmatism. But Hegelianism retained an influence over his philosophical and educational views in a significant way. As we saw in Chapter 1, Hegel's philosophy, according to Dewey, 'supplied a demand for unification that was doubtless an intense emotional craving, and yet was a hunger that only an intellectualized subject-matter could satisfy' (quoted in Westbrook, 1991, p. 14). In what follows in this section, I shall refer simply to the characteristics of this Hegelian position that, in different ways and without the same acceptance of 'absolute idealism', were incorporated into Dewey's philosophical position.

That 'absolute idealism' has the following characteristics.

First, what we perceive is not something independent of our perceiving it. Reality is essentially a mental construction, the product of mind. There is no way of knowing 'the thing in itself'. We need, therefore, to get rid of the separation of 'knower' and 'known', for what is known is part of the knower's mind. Indeed, it would be impossible to think otherwise, because to do so would be to assert a reality that was independent of our perceiving it, despite the fact that there is no logically possible way of stepping outside the mental construct to get at the reality which is not mentally constructed. Furthermore, there is a unity to this 'mental construction of reality'. The general understanding cannot be split up into isolated bits of consciousness. There is coherence in, and a rational structure to, one's worldview. 'The real is rational and the rational is real.' And the function of reason is to grasp more and more the rational within the real. That is what happens as the human organism is constantly overcoming contradictions, and, especially through science, does so systematically and experimentally.

Second, the individual minds were but manifestations of the universal and rational mind (*Geist*). We are not autonomous, independent identities, but share in and are part of a wider human consciousness. The *Geist* is internal to the world. Just as there is no clear separation of 'knower' from 'known', so there is no clear separation of the individual mind from the universal mind or consciousness or reason, in which each participates to a greater or lesser extent. The 'universal mind' is manifested in the consciousness of each.

Third, that universal mind was itself evolving towards self-consciousness – to the recognition of reason in everything. The mind grows through history in what is called a dialectical process. Such a process is a movement between a position of settled belief or harmony (the 'thesis') and a position that contradicts it or creates disharmony (the 'antithesis'), from which would arise a new position or a new harmony of ideas (a higher-level 'synthesis'). To put it much more in Deweyan terms, the settled belief is disturbed by new and incompatible experiences, creating the need for the mental reorganization (or rationalization) of experience to accommodate both the experiences that gave rise to the old belief and the new experiences. And such is a continuous process, because the new synthesis becomes the thesis, which is challenged by a new antithesis, and so it continues. The development through the never-ending resolving of problems constitutes growth. the development of an ever more comprehensive and accommodating organization of experience. It constitutes an ever more consciously rational or coherent grasp of experience. Such a development is intrinsic to the very life of the human organism, since that life is one of always confronting tensions and the breakdown of harmony, which are intrinsic to living.

Fourth, just as individual minds are manifestations of the universal mind evolving to greater degrees of self-consciousness, so those manifestations are embodied in the shared understandings of groups of people – that is, in the culture in which individuals participate and which is preserved in the underlying values and practices of societies and their institutions. Ideas are, as it were, made concrete in specific practices and institutions. F.H. Bradley, the Oxford idealist, referred to 'concrete universals', namely the manifestation of the universal idea in the particular. Each society, therefore, will itself reflect the growing self-consciousness as it realizes the inner contradictions within it, and as it seeks harmony between the often incompatible desires and understandings of the individual minds. Such a society needs to provide the framework of rational thinking through which contradictions can be dealt with and a new synthesis achieved. But an important offshoot of this is that the very ideas which shape our thinking do themselves change as part of the evolving understanding of experience (thereby challenging the analytic tradition within philosophy, which tended to talk about *the* concept of education – or whatever).

Fifth, freedom is to be seen not in the negative sense of not being stopped from following one's desires, but in the positive sense of being able to act in conformity with the rational order of things, this being increasingly understood. The opposite of freedom is enslavement by ignorance, not having control therefore over one's life, being determined by forces that one cannot understand.

These five characteristics of the idealist tradition – first, the mental construction of reality; second, the social nature of that construction; third, the evolving nature of that understanding as the social consciousness in which the individual participates deals with contradictions within it; fourth, the need for communities in which that growth can take place; and finally, the idea of positive freedom – remained a powerful influence on Dewey. This will be explained in the next section.

However, a little more needs to be said about idealism and the nature of its impact on Dewey. It is not a philosophical position that is easy to explain and thus to make plausible on first acquaintance, especially after the devastating attacks that, in England certainly, it received from such philosophers as Bertrand Russell and G.E. Moore (see Russell, 1910, and Moore, 1903). What they attacked was the idealist argument (especially as that was manifest in the writings of Bradley and Green, the Oxford philosophers who influenced Dewey) that the truth of propositions could not be explained by the correspondence of those propositions with reality, something that existed independently of our knowing about it.

In many ways, that 'correspondence theory of truth' seems to be the most commonsense way of understanding 'truth'. 'The cat sat on the mat' is true if there is, independently of my making that statement, an object (which we call 'cat') in a certain position (which we call 'sitting') on another object (which we call 'mat'). Furthermore, we join such statements together with what might be called logical connectives: 'and', 'if', 'not'. Logic, formally speaking, is the science or study of the purely formal relations between propositions. Hence, there are two kinds of true proposition: those that are true simply as a result of following the logical rules, and those that are true because they mirror or correspond to the facts. Language can ultimately be reduced to a large number of basic statements corresponding to the basic facts of reality, joined together by purely logical rules.

However, what came to be called 'the two dogmas of empiricism' (first, the clear distinction between empirical statements and analytic or purely logical statements, and second, the reduction of all empirical statements to basic ones giving a direct report on immediate experience – see Quine, 1961, Chapter 2) were rejected by the idealists for the following reasons. Whatever we say or think has meaning within a system of thought or language. We cannot isolate individual statements and ascertain their truth independently of their meaning within the system as a whole. Furthermore, that system is constantly evolving, as it has to accommodate new experiences. Even the truth of the statement 'the cat sat on the mat' depends on the meaning of the word 'cat', and that meaning changes over time within a changing system of the classification of mammals. The truth of a statement lies partly in its coherence with other statements within a whole system of language, and the system is constantly being transformed. Therefore, there are no *basic* statements, corresponding to a reality as immediately experienced. Rather, there is a system of statements, constantly evolving, through which a coherent and intelligible account of experience is given and through which new experiences are interpreted. We cannot get beyond that account to an 'objective world', objective in the sense that it is independent of our conceiving it and against which our account can be verified or falsified.

The extreme version of this idealist position is called the 'coherence theory of truth' as opposed to the 'correspondence theory of truth'. But the difficulties in such a position are that the stimuli to changing the coherence of the system are not purely internal to the system; the system, as it is, finds that it cannot accommodate new experiences; the system is affected by what is external to the system itself and cannot be controlled by it. Coherence may not be what is meant by truth, but it constitutes a criterion of truth; there is a constant need to be remapping the framework through which we view the world in the light of further experience.

Nonetheless, that constant remapping needs to recognize the internal coherence of the system. It needs to see how ideas interpenetrate – moral and religious, religious and aesthetic, scientific and historical, philosophical and scientific. There is a constant growth of our ideas, arising from all sorts of unpredictable directions. These cannot and should not be fragmented into a multitude of insulated systems; they are interrelated and influence each other. We live in a world of ideas, and those ideas, where they do not cohere together, consequently change in order to resolve the innate tensions between them – reaching a more comprehensive system of synthesis.

Another way into the problem is through what was referred to as the problem of internal–external relations. Take the statement 'Smith met his friend in the pub'. First, who is Smith? One could give a short account. But would that account be sufficient? A sufficient account would require all the relations that Smith has with other people and things. But each of those people and things could be understood fully only in terms of their relations with all they are and have been related to. And so on – until reference has to be made to the whole universe.

In other words, a fragmentary account does not tell the whole truth; the whole or *the* truth would need to embrace an account of the whole universe and the interrelations between the so-called parts. Any finite statement is but a fragment of the truth, and thus only partly true. As a partial truth it is open to yet further correction as new experiences occur or as the system of propositions of which it is a member itself inexorably changes.

Many people would probably find such a position preposterous, no doubt for reasons that were developed philosophically by Russell in his attack on the conflation of internal and external relations. By the distinction between internal and external relations is meant the distinction between those qualities that are essential to a thing or person and those that are merely contingent and accidental. Essential to my identity are such facts about me as when I was born, who my parents are, what I, deep down, believe. What would not seem to be essential are such transient and insignificant factors as what I ate for breakfast this morning or my purchase of a newspaper at the station. In some respects the firm distinction between internal and external relations was entailed by the first 'dogma of empiricism', namely that there is an irreconcilable difference between purely logical statements (around which, if you accept the main thesis of Russell and Whitehead's *Principia Mathematica*, are built mathematical knowledge) and empirical statements whose truth or falsity depends on their correspondence with the facts. But Dewey was not interested in logic in that pure sense – even though the 'father of pragmatism', his uncooperative colleague at Johns Hopkins University, C.S. Peirce, was essentially a logician. *Logic: The Theory of Inquiry*, written by Dewey in 1938, sees logic much more descriptively – that is, as an account of how we in fact think. To separate the form of a statement from its content and use or effect made little sense to him.

However, those who find such a position preposterous should reflect a little on how serious arguments or examinations of controversial situations proceed. One thinks one has understood the situation, but someone suggests, not necessarily new facts, but a reinterpretation of the facts. Under a different set of ideas, the situation as perceived comes to be seen in a different light. Moreover, that reinterpretation takes place possibly within a growing tradition of thinking that previously had not exerted an influence. The 'truth' is as dependent upon the acceptance of a coherent system of ideas as it is upon the discovery of 'facts'. For example, whether or not educational standards have risen or fallen is not a simple fact, verified by reference to test results. It hangs on what is meant by 'education', and 'education' is logically and immediately related to a range of concepts (learning, teaching, indoctrination, conditioning, etc.) within a broader framework of ideas about the life worth living. One's idea of 'education' or of 'being educated' evolves both as a result of what we come to know about 'how we think' (the title of a central text in Dewey's account of education) and as a result of moral considerations about worthwhile goals to be pursued. And in pursuing these questions, we enter into very different philosophical accounts, with constant attempts to reconcile the differences.

Hence, although the absolute idealism of Hegel may be difficult to accept (or indeed to understand), many of the ideas within it were seen as an important antidote to the empiricism that prevailed, and those ideas were absorbed by Dewey. Persons are actively seeking to make sense of experiences as they strive to meet their needs and to solve problems that confront them. Those experiences are made sense of through being connected within the world of ideas; that world of ideas is embodied in the language, the institutions, the social traditions and practices, and the organized bodies of knowledge we have inherited. That world of ideas, however, is itself in a state of change as new experiences challenge old conceptions and as tensions and contradictions within our ideas are overcome. That ever more coherent and comprehensive 'making sense of experience' as we actively strive together to meet and overcome our problems constitutes growth of social understanding and personal development; and that personal development cannot be separated from the wider social understanding of which it is part – the basis of Dewey's understanding of and justification for democracy.

This emphasis on the social nature of growth is important if Dewey is to be distinguished from 'child-centered' philosophers of education with whom he is often associated, to the detriment of his reputation. Sometimes, within the idealist tradition, development lay in the self-realization of the individual. And the growing affirmation of the self was identified with the growing identification of the individual with the whole. For Hegel, both mind and matter were but the manifestations of the spirit growing to self-consciousness. The very influential teacher and education philosopher Froebel, who inspired so many reforms in primary education, subscribed to the Hegelian thesis that the world, as we know it, is permeated by a spiritual unity growing to self-consciousness and that this unity (rather than the apparent diversity) is the proper object of the intellect. Moreover, 'education consists in leading man, as a thinking, intelligent being, growing into self-consciousness, to a pure and unsullied, conscious and free representation of the inner law of Divine Unity, and in teaching him ways and means thereto' (Froebel, 1886, p. 2). The idealism found in Froebel stresses the essential connectedness of things (and of our conceptions of them) and the continuity of the development of our knowledge. Growth through the connectedness of things is the basis of the criticism of the fragmentation of the curriculum and of much learning experience. But the essentially horticultural metaphor of growth to be found in Froebel could lead to exaggerated and dangerously misleading understandings of education which were used to justify questionable educational ('child-centered') practice and which provoked the backlash from the more traditional critics. The horticultural model stresses the similarity between children and plants, each having within themselves the potentiality of becoming 'fully' themselves, of realizing their proper nature, if only they are allowed to mature in the appropriate environment. The Goldsmiths College Curriculum Laboratory (1968), many years ago and following in what it saw to be the footsteps of Froebel, spoke of the teacher watering, re-potting, pruning or simply allowing the children to grow. And there were shades of that in the William Tyndale case referred to on page 36.

But Dewey, although describing education as a process of growth, stressed, unlike Froebel, the essentially social nature of this process. Certainly it is the case that he acknowledged his debt to Hegel's idealism (see Adams and Montague, 1930). To meet the 'demand for unification' it was necessary to transcend the 'divisions and separations' of subject matter that were part of the evolving cultural heritage. It was necessary to make educational sense of 'Hegel's synthesis of subject and object, matter and spirit, the divine and the human' and of his 'dissolution of hard and fast dividing walls' (indeed, of dualisms of any kind). However, that growth is identified with the 'experiential continuum' – with that interconnection of experiences within, and with their transformation by, the social and cultural inheritances which give them meaning, which enable connections to be made and which are preserved in the structures of knowledge we have inherited. There is the identification of the individual with 'the whole' in that there is a seeking for wholeness in the 'experiential continuum' and in that such wholeness is to be found in that world of meaning which has been socially generated.

Pragmatism

In Chapter 3 and subsequently, reference has been made to the philosophical difficulties Dewey found in the various kinds of dualism that dominate our thinking, especially the dualism between mind and body. Difficulties consequently arose over the idea of 'truth' and the verification of what we considered to be true statements. Those within the empirical tradition seemed to be committed to basic statements that somehow mirrored basic facts in the world independent of our perceiving them. On the other hand, there were also difficulties with an idealist position which, in rejecting an unknowable reality independent of our thoughts, saw 'truth' (and thus verification of what we believed) to consist in the inner coherence of our thinking. Pragmatism sought, one might say, a 'middle way' between these two positions. On the one hand, one cannot ignore the experiences that constantly impact upon our thinking, which experiences are not of our making. On the other hand, such experiences do not come, as it were, raw, uninterpreted by the thought-system of the person doing the experiencing. They do not give us direct access to a world independent of our thinking. Furthermore, this 'thinking being' is not awaiting passively for further experiences; he or she is active, seeking perceived goals or ends-in-view, and having to adapt to, and to interpret, experiences as they occur. Pragmatism is, therefore, a philosophical position (loosely described) that pulls all this together, namely people being 'organisms' whose very life is one of actively adapting to an environment in terms of how that environment is conceived and of how it has already affected the capacities of the organism for successful adaptation.

Pragmatism as a philosophy is associated most closely with C.S. Peirce, who was lecturer in philosophy when Dewey undertook his postgraduate studies at Johns Hopkins University. The philosophical position he developed might be best seen through his understanding of four interrelated concepts: those of 'belief', 'truth', 'inquiry', and 'meaning'.

Peirce gave prominence to the state of mind called belief. Belief is the natural condition of the mind, the nature and challenging of which are where philosophy should really begin. That state of belief is challenged by the unsatisfactory feeling of doubt (when, for example, the belief does not produce the outcomes desired). Doubt forces one to further activity in order to resolve the doubt and to return to a state of belief. In other words, unlike Descartes we should not be looking for the foundation of belief as when we decline to believe in 'p' until we can place 'p' on certain and unmistakable foundations. It is simply not possible to doubt everything until such time as we reach secure foundations for belief; life has to go on. Rather should we take beliefs as 'givens' with particular practical functions, and constantly check and reform those beliefs where they fail to function effectively – where they fail to have the practical results required of them.

Indeed, far from the proposition that we believe in being a reflection of a reality to which the proposition corresponds, rather would that proposition have the same meaning as another (which looks quite unlike it) where the belief in either proposition would have the same practical significance. Furthermore, if *any* conceivable consequence is compatible with believing a particular proposition, then for all practical purposes the proposition is meaningless. Many political statements on education are of this nature – like, for example, 'all children are naturally curious'. What conceivable observation could falsify that? There are, of course, similarities in this pragmatic theory of meaning with that of the logical positivists, namely that a statement is meaningless where no conceivable experience or experiment could enable us to check its truth or falsity.

Belief could be conscious, but more often than not it is a disposition or a habit to act in a certain way. To believe that the shop sells bananas means that, given certain conditions and desires, one would act accordingly. Beliefs are embodied in habits, dispositions and spontaneous actions as much as they are in declarations of belief. Indeed, one might say that a person does not really believe in 'p' (for example, that God exists), even when he or she declares it, where that person undertakes no activity that would normally be associated with such a belief (e.g. saying prayers). In other words, beliefs are embodied in the activities or behaviors to which they are normally related. We do not observe the behavior and infer the belief that gives rise to it. There are not two events (my believing and my behaving), but one, namely the one in which the behavior is a reflection of a disposition or belief to act in a certain way in particular circumstances. A belief is to be analyzed in terms of the behavioral consequences of 'holding that belief'.

Beliefs arise in all sorts of ways: from authorities of various kinds, from conversations with others, from one's upbringing, and so on. Their 'truth' lies in the success they have in guiding action, not in their being 'true' reflections of an independent reality. But often they fail to guide successfully. Occurrences that were not anticipated in one's beliefs get in the way. They create a sense of doubt that needs to be overcome. It is in the attempt to eliminate that doubt and to restore belief that one engages in inquiry.

Again, inquiry can take many forms. It can appeal to relevant authorities. It can recall previous and personal experiences. But the most successful kind of inquiry is that of 'scientific method', the systematic suggestion of actions in order to bring about predictable results, and the testing of those suggestions (or hypotheses) against experience. Such systematic exploration of possibilities in order to reach a more settled state of belief does not result in certainty, but only in a justified disposition to act in a certain way until such time as doubt is forced upon one once again.

The theory of meaning behind this needs to be clarified further. A much-quoted passage from Peirce gives a clue: 'Consider what effects, that might conceivably have bearings, we conceive the object of our conception to have. Then, our conception of these effects is the whole of our conceptions of the object' (Peirce, 1877, quoted in Ayer, 1968, p. 49). The meaning of a word is not the object that it designates. The meaning of a statement is not the set of facts to which it is supposed to correspond. Rather, the meaning of the word or statement is the practical effect that the word's or the statement's use has, as that would be understood within the social group within which it is used. What would be initially seen as a description of the object as it is (thick, fragile, etc.) would be really the creation of an effect upon others in terms of the practical expectations arising out of the use of this object. Thick? One would expect it to resist pressure if I were to act upon it in a certain way. Fragile? Then I would expect it to break were I to throw it. A description is more like a hypothesis predicting certain consequences if one were to act in a particular way. The meaning of language lies in the effect it has in creating practical expectations. That, too, shows how the same word can have deceptively different meanings for different people.

Take, for example, the meaning of 'intelligence' within educational discourse. The 'logic of its use' (let us say, as a noun) misleads us often into reacting as though someone has a 'thing' called intelligence, which we can examine and measure. But if we see it as an adjective (as in a phrase Dewey often repeated, 'intelligent action') or in its adverbial sense, then it indicates a certain sort of behavior in particular conditions. Similarly was it the case with certain 'scientific entities' such as atoms. As Noddings (2005, p. 25) points out, they 'existed' for Dewey even though they are invisible, because their 'effects' were reliably observable.

Let us consider the example of the young child learning to speak. The phrases that he or she gradually acquires – 'give me', 'go away', 'I want a biscuit' – have meaning for that child because of the practical effect they generate in other people. Language has meaning as a tool for practical engagement with a problem that needs to be solved. And, indeed, it would be interpreted by the adult in that way. If that is the case with very young children, and with the genesis of language, why should it not be with older people despite the more sophisticated vocabulary and rule-bound nature of their utterances? The grammatical analysis of such rule-bound linguistic behaviors comes much later. People learn how to speak in situations of need – not through, first, studying the grammatical rules of a living language. In a way, Peirce was setting out the underlying logic of language, a logic that is not necessarily reflected in the grammatical rules. Statements that, grammatically, seemed to be categorical were logically analyzed into conditional statements. 'The child is lazy' (categorical) really meant 'If the child were asked to work, he would find excuses to avoid doing so and . . .' (hypothetical or conditional). The full meaning of a statement would be all the possible consequences one might expect if one were to be guided by that statement.

Similarly with propositions. Every proposition that is not purely metaphysical jargon must, within this pragmatic tradition, have some possible bearing on practice, however tenuous that may be. And it was a criticism by some that so much educational theory was meaningless because its 'possible bearing on practice' was hard to discern (see O'Connor, 1956). Indeed, a criticism of Dewey's statement that the aim of education is 'further growth' often follows this line of argument (see Dearden, 1968). And more recent references to aims in terms of 'human flourishing' might be open to the same criticism. What different practical observations can we be expected to make of a flourishing and a non-flourishing child?

On the other hand, there do seem to be some difficulties in the reduction of meaning to 'practical expectations' and to the reduction of all categorical statements to conditional ones. First, for example, the meaning of a shout might be an indication of danger – and a prompt to run away. But such a 'meaning' does not embody a logical or grammatical structure. The practical effect of a shout and of uttering the statement 'I am telling you to run away' might be the same, but the meaning would be significantly different – the first being an utterance that causes an effect, the second embodying both grammatical and logical rules of usage.

Dewey's philosophical position

It is important here to pause awhile to see where we are in the philosophical understanding of the pragmatism which so influenced Dewey.

First, knowledge (as opposed to opinion) is the set of beliefs that are credible, given the inquiries systematically undertaken. There are no solid foundations to such beliefs such that one has grounds for certainty. But belief is 'warranted' because so far, despite rigorous testing, the beliefs continue to provide successful guidance for action.

Second, growth lies in reconciling these different beliefs, in overcoming the contradictions between them as one seeks to make sense of, and to exercise control over, experience. That leads to the greater connectedness of experiences – to a greater sense of wholeness and coherence and to finding unity where once there was fragmentation and tension between the beliefs that one held. This urge for greater unity of understanding was central to Dewey's philosophy and, thus, his educational theory and practice.

Third, those beliefs are related to action in two ways. Their meaning is spelled out in terms of the actions with which they would be associated; they are dispositional. Furthermore, their meaning is related to the inquiry that gave rise to them; they are the product of certain operations on the world. Beliefs, in other words, logically relate to the active inquiry that produced them and to the actions that, in certain conditions, they entail. Educationally, this is critical, because so much of 'education', according to Dewey, disconnected the theories transmitted from the inquiries that gave rise to them and to which they were logically related, and from the practical consequences of subscribing to those theories. They remained, therefore, unintelligible – formulas to be learned for an examination, but not ways of shaping behavior and future expectations.

Fourth, the meaning of what is said or written, which is to be grasped, needs to be related to the sort of experiences that one would expect if one were to believe (rather than simply regurgitate) those theories. And to do that the teacher needs to spell out the meaning of the theories or 'knowledge transmitted' to the experiences, actual or possible, that are meaningful to the young learner.

Fifth, those beliefs are made up of a conceptual organization of experience which itself is constantly changing as it is seen to be inadequate to anticipate future experience or guide future action. For example, one way of understanding science would be to see present ways of understanding the world as a particular phase in our understanding of reality – one that is ever provisional, open to further criticism and reform.

One can see here the difference from prevailing theories of truth and knowledge. These, according to Dewey, had been dominated by the metaphor of the spectator – the mind viewing the world and taking a picture of it. The metaphor for Dewey is, rather, one of the active person internalizing those dispositions and habits that make him or her successfully active. 'Truth' lies not in the correspondence with reality, nor in the coherence of ideas (although that may be a necessary criterion for successful practice), but in warranted guidance for future action. There are no certainties, only more or less credible beliefs in the light of evidence. And, in holding to those beliefs, one should at the same time realize one's fallibility.

On the other hand, it is not the case that Dewey denied there to be a 'world out there'; rather, he believed that we could not know it independently of the way we have come to structure experience. Not any structure would do, because it has to make sense and guide present experience. In doing that, the way of organizing experience constantly comes up against experiences, however interpreted, that are outside our control. The recognition of these is, in a way, the recognition of 'basic' or categorical statements. But even here one must be careful, because such statements are themselves not really basic; they come 'interpreted' and open to revision – even the ones that report our feelings.

The young learner, therefore, comes to the school with his or her own set of beliefs, his or her own internal ways of interpreting the world. From the very start, the child is active in trying to make sense of the world as experienced, acting on the world, giving it sense, exploring its meaning and working out how best to think about it and to act intelligently within it. For teachers to ignore that would be to stick on what is taught – in no way affecting or transforming the consciousness of the learner in a significant way.

Hence, the art of the teacher is to make connections between the inherited way of interpreting experience (in science, for example) and the less mature and less powerful interpretive schemes of the young learner. But the teacher must bear in mind the provisional nature of those inherited forms of interpreting experience. They themselves are developing through experience and criticism, and they often contain within them disagreements among the experts. The teacher is introducing the young learner to a world of ideas, the meaning of which lies in its power to guide action and which is constantly evolving as a result of its failure to do so. Not only does the learner need to appreciate this more pragmatic understanding of meaning, but he or she needs to adopt it, to have respect for his or her provisional state of belief and to be actively seeking to test it against further experience and the recorded experiences and understandings of others who have been there before. Indeed, if one were to talk about *the* aim of education it would be to enable the learner to realize the provisional nature of all his or her beliefs and the possibility of further growth through criticism, which never reaches a final end. But that is a hard lesson to take on board, and to that extent pragmatism is a hard pill to swallow.

Doing philosophy

In the introduction to the 1948 edition of *Reconstruction in Philosophy* (first published in 1920), Dewey states that

> [t]he distinctive office, problems and subject matter of philosophy grow out of stresses and strains in the community life in which a given form of philosophy arises, and that, accordingly, its specific problems vary with the changes in human life that are always going on and that at times constitute a crisis and a turning point in human history.
>
> (RP, 1948, pp. v–vi)

Of course, there are problems, which in one sense are perennial and which constitute the subject matter of philosophical argument: those concerned with knowledge and truth, with the nature of experience and reality, with moral purposes and justification, and with the nature of and relation between the individual and the wider society. Dewey's writings and teaching dealt with these issues, although almost always within the context of education – within the context of enabling young people to grow in accordance with what is distinctive about them.

However, the need for 'reconstruction in philosophy' lay in the fact that how one tackled these issues depended on the background conditions and preoccupations of the society. Classical philosophy – with its understanding of truth and reason, theory and practice, obligation and virtue – reflected the social conditions and relations of the time, namely a society, on the one hand, of an elite that had the freedom and the capacity to contemplate the truth and to acquire 'theory', and, on the other hand, of practical people, ignorant of the principles by which their reality was to be understood, but capable at doing and making. Such a separation of theory from practice was reflected in the consequent moral and political thinking, affecting (among many other things) the education of young people.

The development of the scientific method challenged that classical view. It challenged the separation of theory from practice, of 'pure intellect' from the benefits and challenges of experience. And the reconstruction which Dewey envisaged was that of '[carrying] over into any inquiry into human and moral subjects the kind of method (the method of observation, theory as hypothesis, and experimental test) by which understanding of physical nature has been brought to its present pitch' (RP, 1948, p. ix). Philosophizing, therefore, is to adopt the 'experimental method': hypothesizing and testing, trialing and recognizing error, reformulating in the light of experience, welcoming contrary evidence and criticism, being ever open to revision, formulating but recognizing the provisional nature of any 'warranted assertion', seeking guidance for practice and the management of life, abandoning the search for 'the truth' as such. And this view of, or reconstruction in, philosophy reflects a changed social world shaped by the scientific and technological processes.

Unfortunately, according to Dewey, that 'reconstruction', just as it has yet to permeate philosophical studies themselves (entrenched within either a backwards-looking concern for the problems posed by the classical philosophers of the past or the technical refinements of logic of the present), so too it has hardly touched educational thinking. There, theories are formulated and transmitted in the training and professional development of teachers, totally disconnected from the experience of classrooms and disdainful of the intelligent practice of teachers. Research consists in the application of theory to practice, not the intelligent testing out of ideas in practice and the reformulating of those ideas in the light of experience, albeit provisionally, with a view to more successful if tentative action in the future.

What is needed is not philosophy as a set of theories about truth, knowledge, morality and society, but philosophizing as a way of thinking experimentally about human affairs, especially about the development of the capacity of young people for intelligent adaptation to changing circumstances and to the communities in which they live and to which they should be empowered to contribute.

Indeed, as Noddings argues, 'He [Dewey] insisted that philosophy of education is the most fundamental and important branch of philosophy because all others, in some sense, depend on it. Philosophy of education, for Dewey, was philosophy of life' (2005, p. 25).

Part 4

A Philosopher of Education
for our Time?

Chapter 8

Current Problems and Dewey's 'Would-be Response'

Introduction: 'death and resurrection'

As was explained in the opening chapter of this book, Dewey has frequently been attacked, both in North America and in Britain, as the cause of many of the perceived problems of education. He has been seen as the guru of child-centered education and thereby the enemy of initiation into the different forms of knowledge that are to be transmitted from generation to generation. As Westbrook says, with regard to the United States, 'Dewey's philosophy of education came under heavy attack in the fifties from the opponents of progressive education, who took him to task for virtually everything that was wrong with the American public school system' (Westbrook, 1991, p. 542). But, as Westbrook argues, it was not simply his so-called child-centered ideas about teaching that invited criticism, but also his radical conception of democracy and community, which required the greatest amount of participation of everyone in the decisions that affect their lives. Such democratic ideals were to be nurtured in schools.

Furthermore, Dewey's reputation as a philosopher was greatly diminished. The contrast between his pragmatism and the dominant and positivist form of empiricism, which I referred to in Chapter 3, was such that he could no longer be treated seriously, even though Russell had referred to him earlier as the greatest living American philosopher. Moreover, his idea of 'doing philosophy' hardly supported the burgeoning interest in philosophy as a distinctive discipline, requiring the kind of technical knowledge demanded by editors of philosophical journals. Dewey's idea of 'philosophizing' was to think rigorously about the problem solving that we all have to engage in every day of our lives. As Karl Popper (1999) argued, 'all life is problem solving', and philosophy is that systematic reflection upon how to do it rigorously according to the nature of the question.

Given this demise of Dewey both as a philosopher and as an educationist, how can one suggest that he is the philosopher of education for the twenty-first century?

First, with regard to his reputation as a philosopher, there is a revival of interest in Dewey just as, understandably, the belief in the empiricism that he criticized wanes. Popper's 'evolutionary epistemology' seems more congenial than it would have done half a century ago, and Dewey was certainly an 'evolutionary epistemologist', as I have pointed out in Chapter 7. In the United States there is a renewed interest in pragmatism and thus in philosophizing in the way that Dewey saw it, namely as a way of thinking, neither technical nor esoteric, whereby one might tackle the social issues that confront society at different levels. Indeed, his rejection of 'foundationalism' (that is, that there are knowable and secure foundations upon which knowledge and moral principles can be built) makes him a forerunner of the subsequent postmodern developments that permeate so much educational theory and research.

Two philosophers who have done much to resurrect Dewey's reputation are, in the United States, Richard Rorty, and, in Britain, Alan Ryan. Rorty is so bold as to claim that Dewey is one of 'the three most important philosophers of [the twentieth] century', the other two being Wittgenstein and Heidegger (1979, p. 5). The main reason would seem to be that the main thrust of Dewey's pragmatism was to undermine the traditional analysis of knowledge and reality (to which knowledge is said in some way to correspond) and to develop a pragmatic version of the two, in which there can be no certainties and yet a constructive approach to the future. Dewey showed how it made sense to live without certainty, to have knowledge without firm or certain foundations, and yet to make life better and more livable for as many as possible. And, in so doing and in thinking about the education of young people, he transformed the prevailing view of learning, of inquiring, of 'coming to understand', of 'transmitting knowledge' and thus of schooling.

Ryan, in the final chapter of his book, aptly entitled 'Death and resurrection', similarly points to the temporary demise of Dewey as a philosopher and as a respected educator, but also to the renewed interest and influence. The pragmatic theory of meaning and truth sits comfortably with Habermas's 'ideas about emancipatory forms of social theory', and the significance attached by Habermas to free and equal communication tallies with the emphasis given by Dewey to democratic relations and institutions. As Ryan says, 'the central ideas of *Democracy and Education* can without exaggeration be said to be alive and well seventy-five years later' (1995, p. 357).

What, then, are the main features of Dewey's thinking that make him a candidate for the philosopher of education for the twenty-first century?

Fundamental to Dewey's thinking was his dismissal of the false dualisms that permeated our thinking at the philosophical level and thereby in education: dualisms of mind and matter, of knowledge and experience, of theory and practice, of academic and vocational, of individual fulfillment and social responsibility, of public understanding and private meaning. Education, too often, was focused on the mind disconnected from the body; it was concerned with the transmission of knowledge in a way that ignored the experiences which the learners brought with them to the school. Theory, gained through academic studies, was the mark of the educated person, while practical pursuits were for the vocationally trained. The ultimate aim was the 'educated person' rather than the flourishing community; and public understanding in books was to be acquired without reference to the subjective world of the learner.

On the contrary, argued Dewey, the human person, like any other organism, is constantly and actively adapting to experience and circumstances; those adaptations are made in the light of interpretations of experience; these interpreted experiences then, having been internalized, reinterpret further experience. Such growth through experience, such constant readaptation of how we experience and such further interpretation of experience have no end. They simply lead on to a more competent and fruitful capacity to face and benefit from further experience. Schools were places to assist in that growth of experience, not to ignore it or to leave it at the door of the school as if it were of no consequence. The great barrier to learning, as far as Dewey was concerned, was the 'miseducative experience': the experience, so often engineered at school, that stymied further experience, further growth and further wish to learn, as when the child is bored or put off further learning. Schools, not recognizing this, failed to appreciate the logical connection between the knowledge to be transmitted and the interests and the experiences of young people. They failed to appreciate that the art and role of the teacher lies in the making of these connections – the connections between the personal world of the child and the public world of 'the wisdom of the race'. Schools, implicitly subscribing to such dualisms, would see discipline as being essentially external, and behavior as something to be causally modified. The experiences that the learners bring to the school and that structure their reception of school experience would be ignored as being of no importance.

Furthermore, the circumstances to which the human organism adapts include the organization of experience that has been inherited and is available in books, artifacts, institutional practices, and so on. Therefore, in so adapting, in order to 'manage life intelligently' the human organism must interact with other human beings, and cooperate with them. Thereby, he or she is better able not only to survive but also to gain wider experience and a greater capacity to act intelligently. The social dimension to living is not simply helpful; it is crucial to personal growth, for it is the community with which one interacts in order to reconceptualize how further experience is to be received. But that 'community' need not be a face-to-face community. Nowadays, we hear of 'organic online communities': people who never meet except through the internet. But the world of books and artifacts is a little like that, as people 'communicate' with the stored 'wisdom of the race'. That wisdom relates to the practical issues that the young person is confronted with, and the good teacher is able to make those connections. But that requires all schools to maximize the different strands and flows of communication, to develop the capacities to listen and to take criticism, to nurture the virtues of interrelating and reciprocal support. Schools have to be communities where the opinion of each is of value and where the possibility of growth through the expressing and the challenging of those opinions is paramount. Indeed, that was essential to Dewey's conception of democracy.

Schools therefore should be communities that welcome the experiences young people bring to the school, respect each person's attempt to articulate those experiences, challenge those experiences with other interpretations, develop the capacity to inquire further as a result of these experiences, feed into such inquiries the wisdom of past and present people found in books and artifacts of many sorts (art objects, for instance), and prepare them for facing new experiences and managing their lives in the future. In that broad sense of preparation, all education is vocational.

Problems of our time and a Deweyan response

Each year in England the Chief Inspector of Schools produces an annual report. The report for 2006 judges that 13 percent of secondary schools are inadequate and another 38 percent satisfactory. 'Satisfactory', in inspector-speak, means 'unsatisfactory' in ordinary English. Therefore, half the secondary schools are judged to be 'not good enough'. Those schools judged to be not good enough disproportionately serve areas of disadvantage. A quarter of the pupils in these schools qualified for free school meals. However, the Conservative education spokesman argued that there was a need to concentrate on 'discipline, behaviour and more streaming' (*Guardian*, London, 23 November 2006). And the chief inspector herself said that since the main reason for what is seen to be unsatisfactory 'performance' would appear to be poor leadership, 'we should look at drawing in heads from business and industry' (*The Times*, London, 23 November 2006). What is absent from the report, and indeed from previous ones, which have equally judged schools against the government's or the inspectors' standards, is any questioning of the appropriateness of those standards, of the curriculum by which so many young people and their schools are judged to fail, of an assessment regime that is governed by accountability rather than the improvement of learning, of a selection system that fails rather than respects the struggle to understand, of the implicit rejection of practical learning of the kind that marked the genius of craftsmen such as William Morris and engineers such as Isambard Kingdom Brunel. Rarely are underlying aims of education examined and the values that they incorporate questioned. Perhaps 'failure' lies as much in the disconnection between content and mode of learning, on the one hand, and the perceived relevance of that learning, on the other, as it does on quality of leadership or lack of discipline.

Rarely, too, is the analogy with business examined for its strengths and its weaknesses – the extent to which education can legitimately be conceived as a business. Larry Cuban, in his book *The Blackboard and the Bottom Line: Why Schools Can't Be Businesses* (2004), refers to a successful businessman who, dedicated to improving public schools, told an audience of teachers, 'If I ran my business the way you people operate your schools, I wouldn't be in business very long.' Cross-examined by a teacher, he declared that he selected his blueberries, sending back those that did not meet the high quality he insisted on. To this the teacher replied:

> That's right . . . and we can never send back our blueberries. We take them rich, poor, gifted, exceptional, abused, frightened, confident, homeless, rude, and brilliant. We take them with attention deficit disorder, junior rheumatoid arthritis, and English as their second language. We take them all. Every one. And that . . . is why it is not a business. It's a school.
>
> (Cuban, 2004, p. 4)

Dewey, faced with the disillusioning experience of learning within American schools, and seeing, too, the several attempts to solve the problems as if they were businesses, raised questions about the quality and nature of learning, about the place of the learner's voice in the organization of learning, about the role of subjects as resources for making sense of experience, about the 'common school' and institutional provision of learning, about vocational education and training and about the selection and division of learners into separate groups. And the questions he raised, together with the answers he gave, are as relevant today as they were when, over many years, he wrote about education.

Quality of learning

The overriding purpose of the educational system is to bring about learning. Such a truism seems hardly worth mentioning. However, two questions arise from this truism. The first concerns what counts as having learned something. The second concerns the selection of that which is to be learned. What is worth learning? Strangely, these questions are rarely explored in depth by those who shape the learning experiences of young people.

The difficulty of answering the first lies in the many different things that can be learned: practical skills, concepts, facts, attitudes. What counts as having learned something depends on the logical nature of that which is to be learned. To learn biology is to acquire a grasp of certain key concepts and principles and to know how to apply them. The criteria of having learned successfully (meeting the standards, as it were) depends on the logical structure of the subject matter, and the ability to use this in acting more intelligently in the world. That 'knowing how to apply them' and that being enabled thereby to 'act more intelligently in the world' is central to Dewey's idea of understanding. And, indeed, it is common sense, as well as an important philosophical point about 'understanding'. But despite its commonsense nature, it is little recognized in the definition of standards and in the assessments whereby learners are graded and schools judged to be unsatisfactory. Being able to apply a concept correctly would normally be reflected in practical activities and in being able to recognize instances of the concept. But the severance of theory from practice, the impoverished notion of learning as a matter of learning definitions and formulas and of receiving knowledge that is 'transmitted', militates against proper understanding of key ideas and concepts. The recent Smith Report in the UK, *Making Mathematics Count*, shows how the mastery of mathematical formulas (the ability to see the internal logical structure of the words used, which enables the learner to pass examinations) does not entail an ability to apply these formulas appropriately in 'the real world' (Smith Report, 2004). Dewey would have despaired at the current reduction of fieldwork and coursework in England as an integral part of learning, in order to ensure a more standardized assessment of learning. Writing about

theory does not necessarily show that the learner knows how to apply
that theory, just as writing about 'doing' does not show that the learner
can perform effectively and intelligently. For Dewey, being able to act
appropriately is an essential part of having understood something.
Theory and practice are not set apart; they are different aspects of
'intelligent doing'. The 'high-stakes testing' that has enthralled the
USA and England not only fails to reflect that struggle to understand,
that engagement in inquiry and that making sense of experience, but
also makes these impossible. It becomes an end in itself, an instrument
of accountability based on an impoverished idea of learning.

Furthermore, that 'logical structure' is what we have inherited from
others who have been asking similar questions and pursuing similar
inquiries. In other words, the bodies of knowledge that we seek to
pass on to the next generation are the provisional ways in which we
have organized experience both as a result of inquiry and in order
to guide further inquiry. For Dewey, therefore, inquiry is central to
learning. Learning is achieved through the inquiries of young people,
although informed by the inquiries of others, which Dewey refers to
as the 'accumulated wisdom of the race'. Dewey's distinction between
the 'logical structure of the subject-matter' and the psychology of the
learner, and his idea of 'psychologizing' the former so that it can be
related to the mode of understanding of the latter, are an antidote
to the belief in, and the practice of, the transmission of knowledge
as such, irrespective of the state of mind, the prior knowledge and,
above all, the motivating interests of young people. At best, such
knowledge will be stuck on as if by adhesive, in no way transforming
the understanding of the young person; at worst, the learners will
become totally disengaged from what the school has to offer. To the
chief inspector of schools, Dewey would point out that the unsatisfactory performance of some schools lies in the failure to link what is
to be learned to the deep-down concerns, interests and experiences
of young people. Their voice and their experiences should be at the
centre of curriculum thinking, not something to be harnessed for
motivational purposes in the communication of something they are
not interested in.

Further, inquiry is generally practical. It is pursued in order that
a problem may be solved. Practical engagement with people and

with problems comes up against a problem. The action is stopped temporarily until a possible way forward is conceived. Such practical problem solving can be pursued more or less rigorously, with greater or less relevant background knowledge and with or without the appropriate dispositions and skills. However, under the baleful influence of standards that require theory rather than practice, and the writing about 'doing' rather than the successful doing itself, so practical learning and skills have an ever more diminished place in the curriculum. There is now little room for the experiential and practical learning that engages so many young people, through which an understanding of the world is developed and which, too, was central to Dewey's educational aim of personal growth.

Schools and the institutional provision of learning

The American high school would be seen by many as much more than a place for the transmission of knowledge. The schools tend to be large, reflecting and relating to the local community. Peshkin's case study (1978) of a small town school in the Midwest portrays clearly the importance attached to 'community' – within the school and preparing for the wider community outside the school. Sports events belong as much to the town community as they do to the schools. The visitor from abroad is often surprised to see the scale of the facilities and the significance attached to them.

This contrasts considerably with the experience in England, where extensive areas are affected by selection at the age of 11 and again at 16, and where competition between schools (in order to raise standards) has been actively encouraged by successive governments for the past couple of decades. There has been a history of community schools in Britain (for example, the Cambridge village colleges established by Henry Morris in the 1930s), but this emphasis on the creation of community has never become established in the way that it has in the USA.

For Dewey, schools must be communities if they are to fulfill their educational function, and this for three reasons. First, only in a community will most learners find the appropriate context for learning – the interpersonal communication, criticism, resources and support.

Second, schools were established only because the smaller community of family or locality was no longer able to provide the know-how and skills that were necessary to ensure the intelligent management of their shared interests within the larger interdependent communities. Third, schools were an important element in nurturing the qualities and skills essential for the enhancement and maintenance of the wider community, for, as Dewey states in *Democracy and Education* (p. 81), education has a 'social function, securing direction and development in the immature through their participation in the life of the group to which they belong'. And, as I explained in Chapter 6, the life of the group constitutes a community, where, first, there are shared perceptions of what they have in common and the need to preserve them; second, there is respectful communication between the members of the social group; and third, there are shared aims, beliefs, aspirations, knowledge and understanding.

One should be aware here how different metaphors shape our thinking about schooling. Dewey's metaphor was essentially that of growth, each individual or community respecting the very conditions whereby it might reach its proper end or fulfillment. The socio-biological understanding of growth, through which Dewey viewed human beings, necessarily entailed the involvement of the wider community. Schools were not to be places set apart. But such a metaphorical understanding of schooling was not, nor yet is, universally accepted. The philosopher Michael Oakeshott likens the ideal school to a monastery – to a place set aside where the young learners would not be distracted by the 'business' of everyday life. Far from being linked with or involved with the community, the school should be isolated so that it could pursue, untroubled, its distinctive pursuit of learning. And so many private schools, and indeed new universities, were built in isolated places, turned in on themselves, serving their own communities and preparing their offspring much later to re-enter society, uncontaminated by it and ready thereby to lead it. But Dewey had no truck with Plato's guardian class.

Rather would one expect of a true community, first, the openness to everyone irrespective of class or ability or background, second, within the community, an openness to those deliberations that affect the lives and interests of all its members; third, the involvement of as many as possible in the consequent decision making; fourth, shared activities and responsibilities; fifth, reciprocal support and respect; and sixth, discrimination or selection only when absolutely necessary for the attainment of agreed goals. Such maximum sharing in deliberation, decision making and acceptance of responsibilities was to Dewey the essence of democracy, and a necessary condition for personal growth and fulfillment. The voice of each is of equal importance. He would have condemned the selection that takes place in English schools on grounds of measured intelligence, religious belief or parental choice as subversive of the very aims of education and of a cohesive and vibrant community that would benefit everyone. Cooperation, not competition, was the requirement of a healthy community.

Dewey argued strongly therefore for the 'common school', which would both replicate the community at large and help to create and sustain it. The experiences that young people of diverse backgrounds brought with them to school would enrich each other. The poor would bring the experience of poverty to the rich, who would have, as it were, to make sense of it. The young person of a distinctive religious belief would bring that experience to those studies where consideration is given, in the words of Jerome Bruner (1966), to what it means to be human, how we became so and how we might become more so. The common school was where people of different faiths and backgrounds learned not only to live together (to tolerate differences) but to learn from those differences, to see the weaknesses in their own beliefs and to grow through the interaction with people of different ideas about life. This was even more important where society was constituted of people from many very different cultures, owing to immigration. The common school was the only place where that diversity could be turned into a community of mutual respect which embraced and learned from that diversity.

That was, of course, the ideal of comprehensive schools when they were established in England and Wales in the late 1960s and especially in the 1970s, as was so excellently argued by Daunt (1975) in his book *Comprehensive Values*. If that were the case then, how much more so would it be the case today when, owing to immigration, society seems to be more divided and diverse than ever before. Indeed, it was concluded by the Ouseley Report (2001) into the race riots in

Bradford that, just as a major cause of the riots was the divided school system, which happened as a matter of fact, so a major solution lay in a more integrated schooling for all.

This, however, is not easy to achieve. Communities themselves are often segregated on ethnic and social class lines. The common school for a neighborhood would not very often be one that integrated rather than reinforced diversity. The commitment to faith schools would seem to militate against the idea of the common school. The prevalence of private education in England (affecting approximately 8 percent of generally the more wealthy and privileged population) is yet a further obstacle to a 'common experience'. Indeed, the supporters of faith schools would point to the need for a strong nurturing of young people in the traditions that give them a sense of identity and worth if they are to make a significant contribution to society. As the Chief Rabbi, Jonathan Sacks, argued in relation to the Jewish tradition,

> This is a morality received not made. It is embedded in and reinforced by a total way of life, articulated in texts, transmitted across the generations, enacted in rituals, exemplified by members of the community, and underwritten by revelation and tradition. It has no pretensions to universality. It represents what a Jew must do, in the full knowledge that his Christian neighbours in Mainz are bounded by a different code.
>
> (Sacks, 1997, p. 89)

Each of the communities, therefore, that make up and enrich the larger society is characterized by its own distinctive practices which give it identity and which it seeks to preserve. Those practices, those rituals and symbols, those rules of conduct and relationships, those liturgies and ceremonies, those celebratory feasts and seasons of penance and reflection, capture iconically, enactively and symbolically the beliefs of generations past which cannot be adequately expressed in mere propositions, although it is the task of the theologian and the philosopher to try to do so as much as possible. That preservation of those beliefs, with all the depth of understanding of the human story they portray through the inherited practices and form of life of the community, is central to the education of the next generation, and indeed is seen as an obligation – part of the covenant. Indeed, the significance of that obligation comes across powerfully in *The Politics of Hope*, where Sacks quotes Jacob Neusmer's *Conservative, American and Jewish* thus:

> Civilisation hangs suspended, from generation to generation, by the gossamer thread of memory. If only one cohort of mothers and fathers fails to convey to its children what it has learned from its parents, then the great chain of learning and wisdom snaps. If the guardians of human knowledge stumble only one time, in their fall collapses the whole edifice of knowledge and understanding.
>
> (Sacks, 1997, p. 173)

The advocates of faith schools as against the enforced common school would argue that schools themselves must ensure that the great chain of learning does not snap and that these essentially moral traditions, embedded in social practices and rituals, must be preserved in order to continue to inspire and to inform the common good (see Pring, 2006, for the development of this dilemma between Dewey's idea of the common school and the defense of the voluntary associations to preserve their own distinctive traditions). However, the views of Dewey were clear and unambiguous. As Ryan (1995, p. 339) pointed out, Dewey was strongly opposed to the public support for faith schools, and found himself in conflict with the Catholic Church over this issue. 'Public education was to concentrate on what united American students, not on what divided them.'

With regard to private education, Dewey's way forward would be one of moral persuasion rather than legislation or compulsion. But he would have backed that up with such a resourcing of public education as to make the expenditure on private education unnecessary, if not foolish. And so far as the problems of culturally and materially impoverished neighborhood schools were concerned, he would have applauded the innovations years ago of Midwinter, whose inner-city schools in Liverpool, rather than seeing success to lie in providing a way of escape from the community, would make the experiences and the transformation of the community a central part of the curriculum (see Midwinter, 1975). But, of course, that is partly why Dewey was, and continues to be seen as, a dangerous person. Midwinter's proposals were seen to be a radical challenge to the traditional view of education in which received knowledge is handed down, and where failure is defined in terms of the acceptance or not of that received knowledge. Many challenges of the 1960s and 1970s, which gave a more central voice to the learner as they tried to make sense of their experiences and challenged the values that militated against a sense of community, eventually bit the dust.

Teachers: role, training and professional development

Dewey was particularly damning, as was indicated in Chapter 5, of the diminished role that was afforded to teachers in the traditional education which he so heatedly criticized. The teacher was the person who 'psychologized' the knowledge we have inherited ('the wisdom of the race') so that it helped the young person to make sense of his or her experience – which enabled the young learners to manage their lives more intelligently and to direct them so that they could be open to further enriching experience. To that end, the teacher had to have a foot in both camps: that of the 'logical structure of the subject matter' we have inherited and that of the young learner's interests, aspirations, and modes of understanding. The present preoccupation with the teachers being 'the deliverers of the curriculum' would have been seen as a dangerous nonsense. It would be to deny to the teacher both the role of custodian of the wisdom we have inherited and the role of mediating that wisdom to the particular minds of the learners in his or her charge. Furthermore, the essentially democratic nature of a community simply must include the teacher, the one who is closest to the decisions that affect the quality of learning. The teacher has to be a 'curriculum maker', not a 'curriculum deliverer'.

Such a view seems increasingly alien to the present profession of teaching, and thus to teachers' training and professional development. Standards are laid down centrally as to what teachers should do and achieve, as that is judged by politicians and civil servants without regard to the detailed and specific knowledge of the children to be taught. For Dewey, it made little sense to ignore the individuality of each learner, for each brought with him or her a distinctive set of experiences through which further experience was to be sifted and made sense of. Similarly, the teacher, in helping the learner to make sense of those experiences, would bring his or her own mode of understanding. There is no way, nor should there be, of erasing the dialogic nature of teaching: the meeting of minds between the inexperienced and limited vision of the child and the more sophisticated, experienced and informed mind of the teacher.

That, of course, has implications for the initial training and further professional development of the teacher. Teachers need to be, above all, immersed in the subject matter from which they help young people to make sense of their experiences. They need, too, support in their seeing things from the perspective of the learner. How else can the teacher bridge the gap between the two? Teachers, furthermore, need the opportunity constantly to recharge their batteries – to immerse themselves in the learning from which they can engage with the learners, whose learning they are to enrich. Rather than advocating INSET (in-service training) courses to help teachers meet targets or deliver a curriculum, Dewey would have treated teachers as responsible members of a democratic community engaged in the enrichment of experience, and to that end would have ensured that opportunities were available for them to choose the ways in which they could enrich their experience as a basis for teaching. Heilbronn (2005/6), in one of the few papers that sees the implications of Dewey's philosophy for the education and training of teachers, demonstrates how the knowledge of the teacher (and thus the knowledge to be gained through support of various kinds) is essentially that of practical wisdom based upon experience, which is reflected on systematically and which is interrelated with the research findings which may or may not be seen, in professional judgment, to be relevant. It requires the training of practical judgment as much as the acquaintance with research as such.

Preparation for the world of work: education or training?

The distinction between 'academic' and 'vocational' that presently shapes so much educational thinking (for example, between different kinds of courses for different kinds of people) would make little sense to Dewey. All experience is educational if properly treated – if it becomes a vehicle for further growth and understanding. And all experience that is duly reflected upon and internalized affects how one sees future possibilities and the direction of one's life.

Choosing and being prepared for a specific economic role in life is but one aspect of this intelligent management of life that is the aim of education. 'Vocational training' becomes educational where it encompasses this wider understanding: the grasp of the economic and occupational goals within a wider framework of human fulfill- ment and values. In that sense, as Dewey argues in Chapter 23 of *Democracy and Education*, the whole of education is vocational, and division of learning into academic and vocational introduces yet a further dualism that impoverishes the experiences of both those who are directed up the so-called academic route (marked very often by the absence of practical activities) and those who proceed down the vocational route (marked very often by lack of the broadening influ- ence of the humanities or the understanding of principles behind the work-focused training).

That, however, would mean, for Dewey, not 'a place set apart', a monastic retreat from the world of business. Business, and the eco- nomic life of the community, was an integral part of the experience of all young people and one that they needed to make sense of in the more intelligent management of their lives. Their education should embrace, as Dewey so clearly argued, preparation for living life out- side school, which, of course, includes the world of work into which they are to enter. But for Dewey, 'vocational' has a much broader sense than that of being trained for a specific occupation or specific role.

This too often is not recognized, where, as in the comments of the chief inspector quoted above, 'business' is thought to provide the solution to the problems of education. Cuban describes in detail the ways in which, over the course of a century or more, the business community had perceived its role in the shaping of the content, provision and organization of what happens in schools. But, more importantly, he gets beneath the description to analyze the reasons why the 'business approach' would seem to be appropriate – the 'logic of action', as he calls it. That logic of action consists of clear goals or targets, regular measurement of performance, public knowledge of the results of that measurement, parental choice in the light of that knowledge, competition between a range of providers, performance incentives (e.g. performance-related pay) and sanctions for failure. The underlying philosophy might best be expressed in the McKinsey formula (although Cuban does not make this point): 'What is real can be measured; what can be measured can be controlled.' In some cases the 'logic of action' takes us further – into vouchers, for-profit schools, and the benefits from investment in 'human capital', the economic consequences of which are put forward as an incentive to otherwise reluctant learners.

It is easy, of course, to develop an argument through the contrasting of extreme cases. There are clearly ways in which there need to be connections between the educational system and the economic context in which schools are preparing the next generation of citizens. Well-organized work experience can be educational through the development of understanding, personal qualities and relevant skills. The views of future employers – part of the wider democratic community that has a stake in education – are important, as the teachers prepare young people for the world in which their protégés are to be employed. All this is recognized. But there remain significant differences, as the interrogating teacher pointed out to the seller of blueberry ice cream (see page 166). And the most important difference is the essentially moral purpose of education, an enterprise that is not and cannot be driven by the pursuit of profit. It is not that kind of thing.

The aims of education

Dewey, therefore, would have been horrified at 'the logic of action' and the 'new language' through which the education of young people is now so often described and evaluated – the correlation of 'inputs' to 'outputs' so as to measure 'value added', the 'delivery of a curriculum', the identification of 'performance indicators' which then become the 'learning targets', the use of 'audits' of performance, the talk of 'efficiency gains' where the same 'performance targets' are aimed at with fewer resources. But it would be not only this inappropriate management-speak that would meet his stern disapproval, but also the impoverished language through which young people are described, evaluated and classified – for example, the 'bright' or the 'below average'.

Such language is a major distraction from the moral purposes of education, which, in respect of each person as that person tries to make sense of the physical, social and moral worlds he or she inhabits, is to help them each in their own way to develop a more intelligent grasp of experience. The growing intelligent management of their lives – their growing capacity for 'intelligent action' – will be manifest in different ways. For many, it will require a struggle to understand different aspects of their respective worlds – to make sense of their experiences and to be thereby better prepared to face yet further experiences. But such struggles are too often seen, in the standardized world of public 'education', as being indications of failure rather than occasions for supportive intervention. With so much 'ground to cover' in the transmission of knowledge, there is little room for delay over the idiosyncratic concerns and interests of the individual learner.

Dewey points, therefore, to the quintessentially moral meaning of 'education' at a time when such a moral dimension gets lost in the 'logic of action'. It is easy to be seduced by the understanding of 'education' (going to school, learning this or that subject, becoming numerate) as a means to something else (getting a job, passing examinations) and thus by seeing it as a means to some further end. The overall 'ends', to which 'education' is a means, remain by and large outside the educational debate. 'Education' is assessed more on its 'effectiveness' in its success in attaining preconceived ends. But as was argued in Chapter 3, and as was argued so vigorously by Dewey, 'education' is an evaluative concept. In attributing 'education' to some activities, one is placing a certain value upon them. For Dewey, those values lay in the way in which they enhanced the capacities of the learners to make sense of their respective worlds, to be open to further inquiry and understanding, and to become part of a community of people similarly seeking to improve their understanding and to develop the capacity to work intelligently together. Such 'growth', as he called it, could be supported through acquaintance with what others have thought and said. The art and skill of the teacher are to aid that growth through making such wisdom available at an appropriate level. But ultimately the outcomes of such growth – the cooperative learning within a community – cannot be precisely predicted or predetermined. There are limits to 'central control' both *de facto* and *de jure*.

Perhaps there should be a postscript here upon the nature of educational research. John Elliott has distinguished 'research on education' from 'educational research',

> drawing attention to the difference between viewing research into teaching and learning as a form of ethical inquiry aimed at realising a certain conception of the educational good, and viewing it as a way of constructing knowledge about teaching and learning that is detached from the researcher's own personal constructs of educational value.
>
> (Elliott, 2006)

Both here and elsewhere, Elliott makes reference to Dewey, who would have strongly endorsed this distinction. A theory of inquiry is at the center of Dewey's conception of learning. But it is not only the student who is engaged in constant inquiry as he or she tries to make sense of experience, but also the teacher who is endeavoring to help the learner with that inquiry: when and when not to intervene, what intellectual resources should be brought to bear upon the inquiry, what direction the inquiry should be nudged toward if the learner is to develop yet further capacity to learn and to inquire. The deliberate and thoughtful inquiry into the improvement of learning requires appeal to evidence of different kinds, moral appraisal of consequences, reference to context and the drawing upon experience. It will of course appeal to 'research *on* education', but it is much more than that. It is the practical rather than the technical knowledge (phronesis rather than techne). It is the deliberative 'trying to make sense' in the shaping of action and the intermingling of moral and practical assessments – in fact, 'doing philosophy', as Dewey conceived it.

Conclusion

There remains a consistency throughout Dewey's long life both in his idea of 'doing philosophy', in his criticism and suggested reforms of education, and in the integration of philosophizing and thinking about education. The criticism of 'traditional education', set out in 1897 in 'My pedagogic creed' and provided at the very beginning of this book, survived till the end – and might well serve as an ending to this book. Such traditional education was seen:

- to be disconnected from the experiences that the students brought from their homes and their community
- to be disconnected from the practical and manual activity through which they are engaged with experience
- to ignore the interests that motivate young people to learn
- to treat knowledge as something purely symbolic and formal – organized in textbooks, 'stuck on' without connections to experience or existing ways of understanding
- to maintain discipline through external authority rather than through the engagement of the young people.

The future for Dewey, as indeed it should be for us all, is one where we take the voice and the experience of the young learner seriously, where we explore how the wisdom we have inherited in different forms and packages might help those young people to face the future with greater capability and hope, and to approach this not dogmatically but in the spirit of experiment, tentative conclusions, openness to criticism and openness to all the different voices in our complex society.

References

References to Dewey's works are as follows in chronological order, with the two, three or four letters denoting the abbreviated reference form used in this book. Where there are two dates, the first is that of first publication, the second that of the publication or edition to which reference is made.

Dewey, J. (1889) 'The philosophy of Thomas Hill Green', *Andover Review*, 1: 337–55 **(PTHG)**.

Dewey, J. (1897) 'My pedagogic creed', *School Journal*, 54 (3), reprinted in Garforth, F.W. (1966) *John Dewey: Selected Writings*, London: Heinemann **(MPC)**.

Dewey, J. (1902) *The Child and the Curriculum*, reprinted in Garforth, F.W. (1966) *John Dewey: Selected Writings*, London: Heinemann **(CC)**.

Dewey, J. (1910/1915) *The School and Society*, reprinted in Garforth, F.W. (1966) *John Dewey: Selected Writings*, London: Heinemann **(SS)**.

Dewey, J. (1910/1933) *How We Think*; new edition, Mineola, NY: Dover Publications, 1997 **(HWT)**.

Dewey, J. (1916) *Democracy and Education*, New York: The Free Press **(DE)**.

Dewey, J. (1920/1948) *Reconstruction in Philosophy*, Boston: Beacon Press. Paperback edition 1967 **(RP)**.

Dewey, J. (1922) *Human Nature and Conduct*, New York: Henry Holt **(HNC)**.

Dewey, J. (1925) *Experience and Nature*, Chicago: Open Court **(EN)**.

Dewey, J. (1930) 'From absolutism to experimentalism', in Adams, G.P. and Montague, W.P. (eds) *Contemporary American Philosophy*, vol. 2, London: George Allen & Unwin.

Dewey, J. (1934) *Art as Experience*, New York: Minton, Balch **(AE)**.

Dewey, J. (1934) *A Common Faith*, in Capps, J.M. and Capps, D. (eds) (2005) *James and Dewey on Belief and Experience*, Urbana: University of Illinois Press.

Dewey, J. (1938) *Logic: The Theory of Inquiry*, New York: Holt **(LTI)**.

Dewey, J. (1938) *Experience and Education* **(EE)**.

Other references

Adams, G.P. and Montague, W.P. (1930) (eds) *Contemporary American Philosophy*, vol. 2, London: George Allen & Unwin.

Archambault, R.D. (ed.) (1965) *Philosophical Analysis and Education*, London: Routledge & Kegan Paul.

Auld Report (1976) *William Tyndale Junior and Infant Schools Public Enquiry*, London: HMSO.

Ayer, A.J. (1947) *The Problem of Knowledge*, Harmondsworth, UK: Penguin.

Ayer, A.J. (1947–8) 'Phenomenalism', *Proceedings of the Aristotelian Society*, 47: 163–96.

Ayer, A.J. (1968) *The Origins of Pragmatism*, London: Macmillan.

Bloom, A. (1987) *The Closing of the American Mind*, New York: Simon & Schuster.

Bridges, D. (2003) *Fiction Written under Oath? Essays in Philosophy and Educational Research*, Dordrecht: Kluwer Academic Publishers, 2003.

Bruner, J. (1960) *The Process of Education*, Cambridge, MA: Harvard University Press.

Bruner, J. (1966) 'Man: a course of study', in Bruner, J. *Towards a Theory of Instruction*, Cambridge, MA: Harvard University Press.

Capps, J.M. and Capps, D. (eds) (2005) *James and Dewey on Belief and Experience*, Urbana: University of Illinois Press.

Collings, E. (1923) *An Experiment with a Project Curriculum*, New York: Macmillan.

Cremin, L.A. (1954) *Teachers College*, New York: Teachers College Press.

Cuban, L. (2004) *The Blackboard and the Bottom Line: Why Schools Can't Be Businesses*, Cambridge, MA: Harvard University Press.

Darling, J. (1994) *Child-Centred Education and Its Critics*, London: Paul Chapman.

Daunt, P. (1975) *Comprehensive Values*, London: Heinemann.

Dearden, R.F. (1968) *The Philosophy of Primary Education*, London: Routledge & Kegan Paul.

DfEE (1997) *Education Action Zones: An Introduction*, London: Department for Education and Employment.

Elliott, J. (2006) Paper given at the Annual Conference of the British Educational Research Association, University of Warwick.

Froebel, F. (1886) *The Education of Man*, New York: Appleton Century.

Goldsmiths College Curriculum Laboratory (1968) Report no. 2.

Green, T.H. (1883) *Prolegomena to Ethics*, Oxford: Clarendon Press.

Hadow Report (1932) *The Primary School*, London: HMSO.

Hamlyn, D. (1967) 'The logical and the psychological aspects of learning', in Peters, R.S. (ed.) *The Concept of Education*, London: Routledge & Kegan Paul.

Heilbronn, R. (2005/6) 'The construction of teacher knowledge', *The International Journal of the Humanities*, 3 (1): 129–36.

Her Majesty's Inspectorate (HMI) (1977) *Curriculum 11–16*, London: HMSO.

Hirst, P.H. (1965) 'Liberal education and the nature of knowledge', in Archambault, R.D. (ed.) *Philosophical Analysis and Education*, London: Routledge & Kegan Paul.

Jackson, P.W. (1968) *Life in Classrooms*, New York: Holt, Rinehart & Winston.

James, W. (1904) 'The Chicago School', in Capps, J.M. and Capps, D. (eds) *James and Dewey on Belief and Experience*, Urbana: University of Illinois Press.

Kilpatrick, W.H. (1918) 'The project method', *Teachers College Record*, 19: 319–34.

Kohlberg, L. (1971) 'Stages of moral development as a basis for moral education', in Beck, C.M., Crittenden, B.S. and Sullivan, E.V. (eds) *Moral Education: Interdisciplinary Approaches*, Toronto: University of Toronto Press.

Midwinter, E. (1975) *Education and the Community*, London: Allen & Unwin.

Moore, G.E. (1903) 'The refutation of idealism', *Mind*, 12 (48): 433–53.

Niebuhr, R. (1932) *Moral Man and Immoral Society*, New York: Charles Scribner's Sons.

Noddings, N. (2005) *Philosophy of Education*, 2nd edition, Boulder, CO: Westview Press.

Oakeshott, M. (1972) 'Education: the engagement and its frustration', in Fuller, T. (ed.) (1989) *The Voice of Liberal Learning: Michael Oakeshott on Education*, London: Yale University Press.

Oakeshott, M. (1975) 'A place of learning', in Fuller, T. (ed.) (1989) *The Voice of Liberal Learning: Michael Oakeshott on Education*, London: Yale University Press.

O'Connor, D.J. (1956) *An Introduction to the Philosophy of Education*, London: Routledge & Kegan Paul.

O'Hear, A. (1987) 'The importance of traditional learning', *British Journal of Educational Studies*, 35 (2): 102–14.

O'Hear, A. (1988) Paper given at the Annual Conference of the Society for Applied Philosophy in a symposium on child-centered education.

O'Hear, A. (1991) *Education and Democracy: The Posturing of the Left Establishment*, London: Claridge Press.

Ouseley Report (2001) *Community Pride, not Prejudice*, Bradford: Bradford Local Authority.

Peirce, C.S. (1877) 'How to make our ideas clear', *Popular Science Monthly*, 12: 286–302.

Peshkin, A. (1978) *Growing Up American: Schooling and the Survival of Community*, Chicago: University of Chicago Press.

Peters, R.S. (1965) 'Education as initiation', in Archambault, R.D. (ed.) *Philosophical Analysis and Education*, London: Routledge & Kegan Paul.

Peters, R.S. (1966) *Ethics and Education*, London: George Allen & Unwin.

Peters, R.S. (1977) *Education and the Education of Teachers*, London: Routledge & Kegan Paul.

Peters, R.S. (1981) 'John Dewey's philosophy of education', in *Essays on Educators*, London: Unwin Education Books.

Piaget, J. (1926) *The Language and Thought of the Child*, London: Routledge & Kegan Paul.

Plowden Report (1967) *Children and Their Primary Schools*, London: HMSO.

Popper, K. (1999) *All Life Is Problem Solving*, London: Routledge.

Power, S. and Whitty, G. (1999) 'New Labour's education policy: first, second or third way?', *Journal of Education Policy*, 14 (5): 535–46.

Pring, R. (1989) 'The curriculum and the new vocationalism', *British Journal of Education and Work*, 1 (3): 133–48.

Pring, R. (2006) 'The common school', Memorial Lecture in honor of Professor Terry McLaughlin, November.

Quine, W. (1961) *From a Logical Point of View*, revised edition, Cambridge, MA: Harvard University Press.

Reynolds, D. (1998) 'Teacher effectiveness: better teachers, better schools', *Research Intelligence*, 66: 26–9.

Rorty, R. (1979) *Philosophy and the Mirror of Nature*, Princeton, NJ: Princeton University Press.

Russell, B. (1910) *Philosophical Essays*, London: Longmans, Green.

Russell, B. (1946a) Paper to the Aristotelian Society, partly reproduced in Russell, B. *My Philosophical Development*, 1959.

Russell, B. (1946b) *A History of Western Philosophy*, London: George Allen & Unwin.

Ryan, A. (1995) *John Dewey and the High Tide of American Liberalism*, New York: W.W. Norton.

Ryle, G. (1949) *The Concept of Mind*, London: Hutchinson.

Ryle, G. (ed.) (1956) *The Revolution in Philosophy*, London: Macmillan.

Sacks, J. (1997) *The Politics of Hope*, London: Jonathan Cape.

Scheffler, I. (1960) *The Language of Education*, Springfield, IL: Charles C. Thomas.

Scheffler, I. (1965) 'Is education a discipline?', in Scheffler, I. (ed.) *Philosophy and Education*, Boston: Allyn & Bacon.

Scheffler, I. (1973) *Reason and Teaching*, London: Routledge & Kegan Paul.

Schwab, J.J. (1964) 'Structure of the disciplines: meaning and significance', in Ford, G.W. and Pugno, L. (eds) *The Structure of Knowledge and the Curriculum*, Chicago: Rand McNally.

Simon, B. (1991) *Education and the Social Order 1940–1990*, London: Lawrence & Wishart.

Smith, B.O., Stanley, W.O. and Shores, J.H. (1957) *Fundamentals of Curriculum Development,* New York: Harcourt, Brace & World.

Smith Report (2004) *Making Mathematics Count: The Report of Professor Adrian Smith's Inquiry into Post-14 Mathematics Education,* London: The Stationery Office.

Stenhouse, L. (1975) *Introduction to Curriculum Development and Instruction,* London: Heinemann.

Tawney, R.H. (1938) *Equality,* London: Allen & Unwin.

Westbrook, R.B. (1991) *John Dewey and American Democracy,* Ithaca, NY: Cornell University Press

Wilson, P. (1971) *Interest and Discipline in Education,* London: Routledge & Kegan Paul.

Wilson, P. (1974) 'Interest and discipline in education', *Proceedings of the Philosophy of Education Society of Great Britain,* 8 (2): 181–99.

Index

9 781472 518774